Ein

Tao

For Inner Peace

Illustrated by Mariyana Nikolova
Copy-edited by Chrissy Cutting

Printed by Amazon Kindle Direct Publishing

First print, March 2025

www.einzelganger.co

Thank you supporters and subscribers.

– Einzelgänger

Contents

Introduction

Taoism emerged in China over two thousand years ago and has grown into a vast philosophical and religious tradition. Taoist temples have been built across the world, with various practices having been developed from Taoist thought, such as meditation, qigong, and tai chi. Although today's Taoism is diverse, it generally revolves around getting closer to the Tao—an all-encompassing force that words cannot properly describe. The Tao is shrouded in mystery, and so is its legendary founder, Laozi.

When I first encountered Taoism, its radically different view of the world fascinated me. I was also intrigued by the often poetic and elusive way it conveys wisdom. I was already familiar with Buddhism (which I encountered during my master's in religious studies) and Stoicism, which presented themselves as systems characterized by practical advice and rational explanations of why x leads to y and how to get there. Taoism isn't like that. The Taoist sages don't follow a script. They offer gentle suggestions, paradoxes, and stories. They embody their wisdom. They don't instruct but invite reflection.

The *Tao Te Ching* is widely regarded as the fundamental text of Taoist philosophy. It's a short, poetic work allegedly composed by the sage Laozi (or Lao Tzu) during the late Warring States period (475–221 BCE).

The *Tao Te Ching* blew me away when I first read it. It made me see the world in a totally different light. It showed me how obsessed we are, as a culture, with control and how letting go often achieves more. It also showed me how relative everything is, revealing how if we can look beyond human artificial constructs, we'll see that what we consider good and bad aren't necessarily so.

After reading the *Tao Te Ching*, I explored two other significant Taoist texts: the *Zhuangzi* and the *Liezi*, both named after their respective philosophers. Unlike the *Tao Te Ching*, these story-driven works use rich parables and dialogues to spark the imagination and provoke reflection. They don't offer step-by-step guides on how to become a Taoist or how to get closer to the Tao. But they reveal the folly of what pulls us away from the Tao and subtly point to conditions for a more harmonious existence in alignment with it: simplicity instead of ambition, "non-action" instead of striving, letting go instead of grasping, acceptance instead of resistance.

Taoist texts often carry an element of mockery toward the status quo, or a strictly regulated society, which, back then, was embodied by Confucianism. In many regards, the Taoists take the opposite way. They oppose social conventions. From the Taoist viewpoint, we've lost the Tao if we're immersed in society. Contrary to civilized life, which is governed by all these artificial rules, ethics, morals, customs, and traditions, life in accordance with the Tao lies closer to nature. Thus, a step away from society is a step toward the Tao.

In my opinion, Taoist thought is very relevant to today's societies. Capitalism and consumerism have been major contributors to the rigid ways we see things like happiness, value, purpose, and success. We often base someone's worth on how much money they have. We often equate happiness with the size of our house, bank account, or number of friends. There's a pressure to conform. We must achieve, we must have goals, and we must have a purpose. We even must be happy. All of this leads to a very stressed-out society, where its subjects are devoid of inner peace.

Although I've probably never found the Tao, I have reflected on the Taoist texts, considered their wisdom, examined them closely, and then wrote down my own musings about them. That's what this book has to offer. This isn't an academic work, nor a Taoism 101 containing a systematic explanation of the tradition. These are a collection of writings on Taoist philosophy, originally posted in video format but polished, edited, and occasionally expanded for publishing. Some of the chapters are what I'd call contemporary reflections; others interpret and explain Taoist concepts, such as the "flow state" and "wu wei."

I have used several translations of Taoist texts as sources. For the *Tao Te Ching*, I've primarily used J.H. McDonald's translation; for the *Zhuangzi*, Burton

Watson's; and for the *Liezi*, Eva Wong's creative translation. I've added references in the footnotes. However, for most of the citations from the *Tao Te Ching*, I've added simple references below them in the text (which is a style choice). I've noted any alternative translations in the references.

I hope my reflections give a glimpse of a radically different view of reality that grants a sense of tranquility in these stressful times.

- Einzelgänger

The Wisdom of Letting Go

Letting Go

Mastery of the world is achieved
by letting things take their natural course.
You cannot master the world
by changing the natural way.

Laozi, *Tao Te Ching*, chapter 48

Our civilization is in a state of ongoing striving in which "control" seems to be the highest virtue. You don't have to look far to observe this: in the workplace, for example, employees are more and more controlled and supervised, especially now that employers (the tech overlords) have the technology to do so. Governments are putting increasingly more effort into tracking their citizens, whether it's through camera supervision or the proposal of a so-called "social credit system."

Ironically, the latter is a Chinese invention that seems to go directly against a philosophy that emerged on the same soil: Taoism. As opposed to a control-obsessed society, Taoism revolves around letting go and going with the flow. At first glance, the act of letting go may seem a form of weakness. However, according to the Taoists, by achieving a correct understanding of how the universe works, we can approach life more intelligently, more efficiently, and go with the flow rather than swimming against it. Therefore, the power of letting go is a form of strength based on sophistication rather than force.

There are countless ways in which we can interpret the main Taoist scripture: the *Tao Te Ching*. One way is to see it as a guide for a ruler. What characterizes its passages regarding governance is that Laozi puts emphasis on ruling by "not ruling," as he compared governing a country with frying a small fish: too much poking spoils the meat. He argued that when a ruler tightens his grip on the people, all kinds of negative side effects will occur. You'll see that people become distrustful toward one another when the government is too patronizing, and when it's too intrusive, people become rebellious. But when a leader is unobtrusive and acts with integrity, then people will become whole, as they're granted the space to naturally evolve.

It's clear that Laozi favors a passive form of governance, which doesn't just apply to ruling a state but also to the governance of ourselves. Because letting things go is key to letting nature do the work, which applies to any level. Let's explore several Taoist ideas that show the power of letting go.

1) Non-doing

The Taoist concept of *wu wei* can be explained as "effortless action," or the so-called "flow state," but also as "non-doing," or "knowing when to act and when not to." (See chapter "Wu Wei" for an in-depth exploration.) When you take a critical look at yourself, you may see an incessant desire for control in many areas of your life. You may feel the need to control your pets, children, gardens, video games, (in some cases) partners, and first and foremost: your future. Now, control isn't always a bad thing. In order to survive, exerting influence on the environment is necessary to some extent. Self-control, in particular, can lead one in a positive direction. Without control, human civilization would probably never have occurred. But too much of it doesn't get us anywhere.

It seems that we systematically underrate the natural influences that lie at the basis of our daily lives. We can't control everything, and many things happen when we stop controlling them. Let's look at trees, for example. We can plant a tree, water it, add some fertilizer, and make sure it's exposed to enough sunlight. However, any more intervention would only damage the process because we would be interrupting nature and preventing it from doing its job. Another example is attraction. The first step to attracting someone is simply showing ourselves so that the person we want to attract knows that we exist. Then, attraction either happens or not.

When the attraction is there, you could easily blow it by taking too much action. Attraction is a natural phenomenon that is beyond our control. It absolutely cannot be enforced. Instead, it has to grow or erupt spontaneously. And there's only one way to let the seed of attraction grow into a beautiful tree, and that is *not intervening*, aside from occasional watering. Silence makes the heart grow fonder. That's why "letting go" is crucial in relationships. By letting go, you give space for your partner's attraction to develop and flourish.

2) Embracing change

The Taoists were aware that life unfolds in a constant movement between opposites: between high and low, light and dark, yin and yang. There isn't much we can do about it, and the most efficient way of living is simply moving along with the waves of existence. The flow of life and its transformations are inevitable.

Yet, we see so many people clinging to their circumstances. In the metaphor of the river stream, they hold on tightly to a branch or rock, afraid to let go, because they want complete control over their position. They simply don't trust the way life unfolds; they think that if they don't exert control, everything will fall apart. The consequence of this attitude? A rigid and anxious life. They see life passing them by, including many opportunities for positive change, and they miss out on a lot of fun. As Laozi wrote:

The living are soft and yielding;
the dead are rigid and stiff.
Living plants are flexible and tender;
the dead are brittle and dry.

Laozi, *Tao Te Ching*, chapter 76

There are also those who swim against the stream. They're the biggest energy wasters of them all. Perhaps they see honor and virtue in taking an extremely non-agreeable stance in life. Nonetheless, exercising constant resistance to how things unfold is an exhausting way to live. Also, it may not get them anywhere, as they've been standing in their own way.

Through non-acceptance of "how things are," people end up fighting themselves. Because of certain societal expectations, people engage in a battle against their inherent nature instead of flowing along with the attributes that nature has given them. We could say, *"Follow your strength instead of trying to repair your weakness."*

Embracing change also applies to uselessness and usefulness. The sage Zhuangzi observed that usefulness depends on the circumstances, as he talked about a merchant who tried to sell shirts to a tribe[1] whose members were covered in tattoos and always showed them off by walking around shirtless. To them, shirts are useless. But to us (at least most of us), they aren't useless at all.

Usefulness and uselessness are relative and are not to be treated with rigidity. When you live in New

---

[1] You can find this story in *Zhuangzi*, Inner Chapters, Chapter 1: Carefree Living

York, for example, having a car is less useful than when you live somewhere in the countryside where the next village is fifty miles away. So, we ought to be willing to let go of things that are *useless in one situation* and adopt what's *useful* instead. That's how we make change an ally and not an enemy.

3) Not focusing on outcomes

Comparable to the Stoics, the Taoists observed that the focus on future outcomes has a negative effect on us. Focusing too much on the future makes us anxious. Our present endeavors become fueled by a desire for an uncontrollable result, and the more we crave that, the less we value the present moment: the place we live and experience.

Zhuangzi goes one step further by telling us that the more we value something external, the worse we perform in the present. He tells us about an archer who loses his ability to shoot when he focuses too much on the prize.

He who is contending for a piece of earthenware puts forth all his skill. If the prize be a buckle of brass, he shoots timorously; if it be for an article of gold, he shoots as if he were blind. The skill of the archer is the same in all the cases; but (in the two latter cases) he is under the influence of solicitude, and looks on the external prize as most important. All who attach importance to what is external show stupidity in themselves.[2]

This doesn't mean that people who want external things are stupid. It means that when our minds are in the future, we paralyze ourselves in the present, the moment we can actually work on attaining whatever goal we have. This principle lies at the basis of the "flow state" that we see in activities like sports, art, and dancing (see chapter "Flow"). When we experience this flow state, we're so immersed in the task at hand that we completely forget about the future. It's like the dance dances itself.

4) Letting go of excess

In a society where status is the ultimate concern, everyone wants to be at the top. Not because it's necessarily the best place to be, but because we've collectively decided that high status is preferable and low status is horrible. This also comes with a collective pursuit of the former and a collective aversion to the latter.

But the tallest trees catch the most wind. When you're at the top of the hierarchy, it takes a tremendous amount of effort to stay there because everyone wants to take your position. It's stressful compared to the lower positions, in which one lives more privately, with less

---

[2] *Zhuangzi*, Outer Chapters, Chapter 19: The Full Understanding of Life

competition, fewer enemies, and, in general, less effort. The other extreme, however, is a place of deprivation. If we deliberately seek the absolute bottom, we become ascetics. Although there's still a strong attachment, it comes in a different form: the attachment is to deprivation (and whatever spiritual goals we want to achieve by doing this).

The question we can ask ourselves is: *What do we truly need?* Zhuangzi observed that a bird that nests in the forest wants no more than one branch. And that a mole that drinks from the pond drinks no more than a bellyful.[3] So, if we aim for what we need and let go of excess, we prevent possessions from becoming our prison cell, which allows us to travel light.

The ancient Greek philosopher Epicurus also observed that the basic necessities for life are easy to come by and that living moderately is the key to happiness. It's a path that's easy and sustainable. As Laozi wrote: *"Those who use moderation are already on the path to the Tao."*

When we stop striving, we give nature space to unfold. In trusting the universe and accepting that it is ever-changing lies the opportunity to become loose and supple instead of rigid and brittle. The power of letting go means that we float along the stream without grasping for

---

[3] *Zhuangzi*, Inner Chapters, Chapter 1: Chapter 1: Carefree Living

rocks and branches and that we cut loose dead weight so we can navigate through life with minimal effort.

Not Worrying

Our busy lives often lead to feelings of stress, exhaustion, and even burnout. Stress is one of the major causes of illness and can also lead to depression and anxiety. Luckily, the writings of ancient Taoist sages offer plenty of philosophical ideas that may help us to relieve stress and reduce our endless worries.

From a Taoist viewpoint, we go against the natural course as soon as we try to *force* things. Forcing means interfering with or even going against nature, which only brings about trouble, according to the Taoists. Looking at many of today's societies, we see ourselves continually forcing our way through life. We not only seek to alter nature to our own liking but also to control things we have essentially no control over, like fate and external circumstances. We're obsessed with *control.* And the Taoist sages teach the opposite: *letting go.*

As mentioned before, letting go is a recurring theme in Taoist philosophy. Laozi reminds us of how nature takes care of itself and that, without interference, everything gets done. Liezi, the lesser-known sage, observed how obsessed we are with finding happiness in the outside world and that our efforts to achieve it and our clinging to external circumstances make us miserable. We're unwilling to let go of our restless pursuit of being happy, which is precisely the reason why we aren't. In reality, our efforts not to be unhappy generate the unpleasant feeling that we are trying to escape.

The writings of the ancient Taoists persuade us to go in a different direction: we ought to let go of existing concepts and worldviews, become aware of emptiness, let nature take its course, and move with nature rather than against it. The goal? An easier life, less worrying, and following Tao, the universal principle. This chapter explores ancient Taoist ideas that may serve as antidotes for reducing worry in a world out of control.

1) Leaving things alone

Zhuangzi knew how to do nothing. He didn't interfere with natural processes because if he did, nature would blow out of shape and become something it wasn't. He left things alone, running their natural course, and saw things grow ripe around him.

In many present-day cultures obsessed with achievement and productivity, "doing nothing" is considered a sin. We don't allow ourselves to "do nothing," as we should always be busy. We prefer to work against nature over not working at all, even if our efforts only interfere with what we are trying to achieve.

In the chapter "Wu Wei," you'll find an example of a farmer pulling his crops to make them grow faster to no avail; he even damages his crops in the process. Similarly, we push and pull wherever we can, often without results, sometimes even sabotaging our progress, leading to stress and exhaustion and increasing our worries.

When we leave things alone, we respect their natural course. Our environment doesn't always need our interference, whether at work or home. Problems often solve themselves, and life always falls into place eventually, regardless of whether we like the outcome or not. What seems like lousy luck may be a blessing in disguise, and what we try to accomplish may turn out to be a curse. Moreover, the universe always gets its way, so attempting to control it is futile.

2) Stop looking for happiness

Zhuangzi couldn't tell if what all those busy people chased after was happiness or not. But he could see that their ways of trying to obtain it made them miserable. People were stressed, always in a rush in their obsessive search for happiness; their faces looked tired and grim.

If the chasing of happiness makes our lives bleak, we might as well stop it, argued Zhuangzi. We not only exhaust ourselves, but we also don't get what we're looking for and thus end up in a lose–lose situation. Things like wealth and fame might be fun for a while but only come with new worries in the long run because as soon as we've obtained these pleasures, we fear losing them. Zhuangzi stated:

Those who think that wealth is the proper thing for them cannot give up their revenues; those who seek distinction cannot give up the thought of fame; those who cleave to power cannot give the handle of it to others. While they hold their grasp of those things, they are afraid (of losing them). When they let them go, they are grieved; and they will not look at a single example, from which they might perceive the (folly) of their restless pursuits: such men are under the doom of Heaven.[4]

Zhuangzi argued that contentment and well-being become possible if we stop acting with them in view. If we don't desire happiness and well-being, the "wrong" of not having what we want and the "right" of getting what we wish disappear. And thus, we don't worry about getting (or not getting) happiness. Instead, we enjoy happiness because we have stopped caring about obtaining it.

3) Seeing the emptiness

Liezi argued that people generally like to be praised, as they feel good when others recognize their accomplishments. But Liezi valued *emptiness* instead, as he explained that we're less stressed when empty of all these attachments. We'll have fewer things to worry about

---

[4] *Zhuangzi*, Outer Chapters, The Revolution of Heaven

if we don't care so much about other people's approval and validation.

Liezi said that we seek to receive credit for things that aren't entirely our own doing. Many of the things that people praise us for depend on the right circumstances or inborn characteristics. If the conditions are right, our actions only *contribute* to the result, as many other factors play their part. For example, people who receive praise as Instagram models receive it primarily for having good genetics and adhering to current beauty standards. So, what accomplishment is genuinely their own? Instead of worrying about obtaining "praise" that ultimately doesn't belong to anyone, Liezi urges us to quiet down and let go:

Seeing the emptiness of things can help us cultivate stillness and peace of mind. If you do not know how to keep still in this crazy world, you will be drawn into all kinds of unnecessary trouble.[5]

Many things we chase are empty; there's nothing to them except the value we attribute to them. Praise is empty. And often (if not always), it's not even deserved. The same goes for many other pursuits we deem significant but are pretty meaningless. It's like we engage in them just to divert ourselves from the emptiness of it

[5] Wong, Eva. *Lieh-tzu: A Taoist Guide to Practical Living (Shambhala Dragon Editions)* (p. 54). Shambhala.

all. But if we'd embrace this emptiness, accept it, and let go of all these games, the chasing, the rat races, the continual quest for happiness, we'd be better off, according to Liezi.

4) The inner law

By continually stretching ourselves beyond our capacities, we ask for trouble, so thought Laozi. He wrote that those who stand on tiptoes do not stand firmly, and those who rush ahead don't get very far.[6]

Standing on tiptoes occurs if we try to extend our control over things we cannot control, so argued Zhuangzi. The book *The Way of Chuang Tzu* (a collection of poetic renderings by Trappist monk Thomas Merton) explains the difference between someone *"whose law is within himself"* and someone *"whose law is outside himself."* The first person acts without being influenced by the approval and disapproval of others. The second person is directed by things outside his control and thus becomes a plaything of his circumstances. Whatever happens in the outside world decides his mood.

"When he tries to extend his power over objects, those objects gain control over him,"[7] said Zhuangzi. When things go well, he's happy and content. When things don't go well, he's unhappy and full of worry. And

---

[6] Laozi, *Tao Te Ching*, chapter 24

[7] Thomas Merton, *The Way of Chuang Tzu*, The Inner Law

thus, he tries to get what he wants and avoid what he doesn't want, always concerned with a universe he ultimately cannot control.

He who seeks to extend his control
Is nothing but an operator
While he thinks he is
Surpassing others,
Others see him merely
Straining, stretching,
To stand on tiptoe.[8]

One of the lessons we can learn from Zhuangzi's writings is to avert our attention and desire from the outside world and turn it within. Ultimately, it's not the world that decides how we feel but our minds. Therefore, if we seek contentment, adjusting our minds makes more sense than attempting to control our environment. Everything around us is out of control. But we *do* have control over our thoughts, choices, and attitudes toward the environment. The less we seek contentment outside ourselves, the less we must stand on our tiptoes to obtain it.

5) Not worrying about "fate"

---

[8] Thomas Merton, *The Way of Chuang Tzu*, The Inner Law

Zhuangzi observed that not fate itself but worrying *about* fate gets people in trouble. An archer, for example, may shoot perfectly during practice but horribly when he competes for a prize. As soon as we desire a specific outcome, we worry about not achieving it. The archer of Zhuangzi's story[9] shoots just fine if he only shoots for the sake of shooting. But when there's a prize in his view, he starts caring more, even though his skill hasn't changed. "He thinks more of winning than of shooting. And the need to win drains him of power," Zhuangzi stated.

So, how should we handle fate? How do we treat an uncertain future with the possibility of fortune or misfortune? Liezi tells us about an older man from the kingdom of Chi who was afraid that the sky would fall and the earth would break up.[10] And who worried that if it happened, he'd have no place to run, and his death would be unavoidable. So, a friend tried to calm him down by assuring him that the sky wouldn't fall, so there was nothing to worry about. Then, a sage told him there *is,* in fact, a possibility of the sky falling, although the chances are small, so the elder shouldn't be too concerned.

Liezi chuckled and said:

---

[9] You'll find this story in *Zhuangzi*, Outer Chapters, Chapter 19: Mastering Life

[10] You'll find this story in the book *Lieh-Tzu: A Practical Guide to Taoist Living* by Eva Wong, chapter 10: Worrying that the sky will fall

It's nonsense even to think about whether heaven and earth can or cannot be destroyed. Whether they will perish or not is something we don't know. If heaven and earth will not perish, that's great. We can live our lives without worry. However, if they will perish, that's something we can't do much about, so why worry about it?[11]

The old Taoist sage stated that there's no point in occupying ourselves with the question of whether or not the earth will perish. It's something completely out of our control. If it happens, it happens. Moreover, we don't even know what this fate we fear entails exactly. What's it like to be dead? Or, for example, what happens after we lose our jobs or our marriages end? We assume these happenings are disasters, even though they could be blessings in disguise. Again, whatever happens, it's out of our control anyway, so worrying about it is a waste of time.

---

[11] Wong, Eva. *Lieh-tzu: A Taoist Guide to Practical Living (Shambhala Dragon Editions)* (p. 58). Shambhala. Kindle Edition.

Heartbreak

Taoist philosophy emphasizes letting go, accepting, yielding, and going with the flow. All Taoist sages seem to agree that it's better not to force, allow change to happen, and move along with life's constant transformations than to resist change and cling to what's already in the past.

When we are romantically involved with someone, we often see the opposite happening of what the Taoists teach. We attach, we cling, we control, and we're usually very fearful of being abandoned by the person who seems to fill the hole in our hearts. At the peak of the "honeymoon phase," when everything feels carefree and joyful, we wish it would last forever. But as we all know, this period of mutual infatuation rarely lasts.

No feeling is final. The changing nature of our emotional world causes us to fall out of love, sometimes as quickly as we fall in love. When feelings change, the relationship changes. Frequently, the consequence of deteriorated feelings of attraction, for whatever reason, is a breakup.

Such a drastic change is challenging to handle, especially when the decline in attraction isn't mutual. For some, it takes years (or even a lifetime) to get over someone. Others never truly accept the breakup and move heaven and earth to win back their old flame, to no avail.

When we cannot change outside circumstances, the only way to move forward is to change *ourselves*, including how we look at the situation at hand. The Taoist ideas in this chapter could help to see heartbreak in another light.

1) Holding on, letting go

The art of letting go is a recurring theme in Taoist texts. In the book of *Zhuangzi*, we find a short story about Pei Kung She, the tax collector. In order to make a set of new bells for the king, he had to collect sufficient taxes. What seemed an impossible task, Pei finished without effort, and within three months, the bells were completed.

The king asked: *"Master Pei, what is this art you wield?"*

Then, Pei explained that he didn't wield anything.

Mysteriously, wonderfully, I bid farewell to what goes, I greet what comes; for what comes cannot be denied, and what goes cannot be detained. I follow the rude and violent, trail after the meek and bending, letting each come to its own end. So I can collect taxes from morning to night and meet not the slightest rebuff.[12]

---

[12] *Zhuangzi*, Outer Chapters, Chapter 20: The Mountain Tree

Master Pei didn't force anything and got great results. He didn't get into arguments and simply bent with the situations he encountered.

This story has nothing to do with breakups so far. But it reflects the Taoist way of life—flowing with change and letting go of what passes—an attitude that is the opposite of how people generally approach romantic love. Instead of letting go, we tend to grasp. When we lose someone we're attached to, we resist change, denying the present and clinging to the past. But by doing so, we're opposing the ways of nature, so to speak. Not only do we act in opposition to the outside world, but also to ourselves. If we let go, we are soft and supple. If we refuse to let go, we are dry and brittle. From a Taoist point of view, life is soft and supple; death is brittle and dry.[13]

Imagine the hurt caused by the unwillingness to let go of what's already passed. When we keep living in the past, we'll eventually become bitter and unable to allow the present in our lives. Like a river flowing past someone tightly clinging to a rock, life passes by someone refusing to let go of a past relationship. What a waste, as life contains so many opportunities that we cannot see because we've turned our backs on them. When we don't bid farewell to what goes, we seem to be less likely to greet what comes. Because as long as we don't let go of one thing, it's impossible to embrace another fully.

---

[13] Referring to Laozi's famous words in the *Tao Te Ching*, chapter 76

2) A blessing in disguise

Once upon a time, Zhuangzi wandered in the mountains and encountered an enormous tree.[14] Its branches were thick and crooked. A lumberjack passed by but refused to cut down the crooked tree. When Zhuangzi asked him why, he replied: *"There's nothing this tree could be used for! It's worthless!"*

But Zhuangzi said: *"Well, because of its worthlessness, this tree can live out the years Heaven gave it."*

Again, the story itself may have nothing to do with heartbreak, but there's a lesson to be learned about the blessing of rejection. The woodcutter rejected the tree because it wasn't good enough in his eyes. But this rejection allowed the tree to grow old and beautiful, and over the years, people came to admire it and even declared it a holy place.

Someone rejecting us is just another change that comes with loss but also with gain. Take, for example, the many benefits of being single regarding personal growth, finding meaning in life, and tranquility. And the calmness that's available to us after an emotionally draining relationship ends can be recuperative. We may also come to see that we're not compatible with the person we

---

[14] *Zhuangzi*, Outer Chapters, Chapter 20: The Mountain Tree

struggle to let go of, and perhaps we're designed for another path that better suits our nature.

The crooked tree shows us that not all trees are fit to be turned into wooden planks. Likewise, not all people are suitable for each other. And for some, it may even be better to remain single in certain situations. The crooked tree simply followed its nature; it became what it naturally would become: useless from one perspective but still valuable in the eyes of others.

In accepting the end of a relationship and letting go of someone, we also follow the way nature (or fate) intends, which is that the person we were once romantically involved with goes another way. As we've learned from the crooked tree: everything has a part to play in this universe. And the roles we've played in the lives of the people we've lost (how unfortunate this may seem) are over.

3) Embracing impermanence

After letting ourselves become attached to another person, there's often no way to eradicate this attachment overnight. What resists, persists, and the more we fight the pain caused by separation, the more painful it becomes.

The attachments that develop between people who are romantically involved are often deep and stubborn. Such a bond either dissolves slowly over time, or it's ripped apart by sudden separation. The latter is painful: the more we attach, the more we grow into each other, the more drastic the breakup is. When this separation happens, there's a wound that needs time to heal. Many people try to accelerate this process by seeking distractions and repressing thoughts and emotions, but to no avail, as the wound heals at a natural pace.

We can choose to keep running from our pain, but we'll have to face it someday, often when we don't expect it. We can choose to fight our pain, but by doing so, it only increases because we put an extra layer of pain on top of the pain that already exists. The more we want to be free of pain, the more pain we experience. So, instead of trying to get rid of the pain that comes with letting someone go, we can accept it as an inevitable part of a breakup until it naturally subsides, like cloudiness naturally transforms into a clear sky.

Mastery of the world is achieved
by letting things take their natural course.
You cannot master the world
by changing the natural way.

Laozi, *Tao Te Ching*, 48

The beauty is that we can trust time to solve the problems that we cannot solve ourselves. Even though change seems to work against us when we lose someone we love, it also works to our advantage as it will eventually rid us of our grief and sorrow. This process itself has valuable things to offer, like becoming familiar with pain, which is the root of compassion and empathy, as we learn how people feel in situations that we've been through ourselves. Moreover, the pain of heartbreak has been a source of inspiration for many artists.

Impermanence can be a friend or foe, depending on how we treat it. If we continually move in opposition to it, our suffering will be endless. But if we allow it to be, we will enable it to dissolve naturally, and we won't suffer the additional pain that comes with resisting what is.

Letting someone go can be a never-ending, painful process if we refuse to move along with the changing nature of the universe. Nothing is permanent. Everything comes and goes, including the people in our lives. Life isn't supposed to play out the way we want, but the way it happens. From a Taoist perspective, nothing that happens is fundamentally wrong or right; it's simply the universe changing. But it's the mind that adds problematic elements to some of these changes, making them undesirable in our eyes. So, we don't suffer change itself, but the way we look at it.

A Taoist sage greets what comes and says farewell to what goes. Change is the natural state of the universe; it moves like the sea's tides, between opposites like ebb and flow, high and low, front and back. If we are supple and flexible toward change, we may start to enjoy the way things are at the moment and accept their impermanent nature. A breakup, then, isn't right or wrong but rather just another change that we can ride like an ocean's wave.

Drunk On Life

The habit of drinking is deeply ingrained in Western culture. Being drunk is often seen as an enjoyable state in which our sorrows are washed away and exchanged for courage and an extraordinary ability to be merry and happy. Yes, alcohol loosens our inhibitions, dissolves our fears, and makes us forget about our problems—at least for a while. But it also dampens the senses, reduces our mental capabilities, impairs our motor skills, and basically helps us to make fools of ourselves. Moreover, drunkenness often leads to violence, and the trap of alcoholism has been destroying millions of lives.

Thus, we might choose the risky joy of drinking, but the overall debilitating effects of doing so prevent us from truly immersing ourselves in the precious gift that the universe has given to us: *life*. Instead of escaping the experience of life, in all its rawness, with all its emotional highs and lows, its joys and hardships, can't we just enjoy life as it comes, soberly, as much as we enjoy the state of drunkenness? Or simply put: *How can we get drunk on life?*

Years ago, I stumbled upon a Taoist tale[15] about Laozi meeting up with Confucius and Buddha in a

---

[15] I've got this story from a YouTube video by "ruzickaw:" ruzickaw. (2011, March 30). *Taoist tales LAO TZU , BUDDHA , CONFUCIUS AND THE JUICE OF LIFE* [Video]. YouTube. https://www.youtube.com/watch?v=-o_KD9A2pAQ

teahouse. When they were sitting together at a table, the waiter offered them a special drink called "the juice of life." Immediately, Buddha rejected this, saying that birth, death, and life are all suffering and that a drink called "the juice of life" is definitely not worth taking. As a matter of fact, his enlightenment meant freedom from the wheel of suffering. So why should he masochistically administer the pain that he wanted to escape?

Confucius then said that he couldn't judge the drink before he tasted it. He took a sip but didn't like the taste *at all*. "Buddha, you're right!" he said. "It's foul, it's bitter, it's miserable, it's not worth drinking." Then, Laozi took the bottle and drank it in one go. After that, he got up and started to dance, and dance, and dance, while screaming like a madman. After a while, he stopped and returned to his seat. Buddha and Confucius became curious and asked, "So, how was it?"

Laozi answered: "I'm not going to say a word because there's nothing to be said." The sage explained that Buddha was too quick to judge, and Confucius was too rash for judging based on a small sip. In theory, they might be right: that life isn't worth the suffering. And based on their doctrines, it might be better to avoid certain elements of life in order to avoid suffering. But in the story, they refuse to experience life. And a million words are not enough to describe what it really is to be alive.

Hence: "There's nothing to be said." To really judge about life, one has to fully experience it.

Not to discredit Buddha or Confucius and their traditions, which (needless to say) contain profound wisdom, the story offers two important messages. The first one is not to take religions or ideologies *so* seriously that they block us from experiencing life. When the rules we impose on ourselves are too rigid and inflexible, it's difficult to move along with existence, which is always in flux. As Laozi wrote in the *Tao Te Ching*:

Those who are stiff and rigid
are the disciples of death.
Those who are soft and yielding
are the disciples of life.

Laozi, *Tao Te Ching,* chapter 76

The second one is that to experience life, we should drink it all at once and just dance. We're likely inclined to dance after drinking a lot of alcoholic beverages. Without a doubt, drunkenness by substances is an experience that many people regard as a joie de vivre. But, paradoxically, the basis for this joy lies in closing ourselves off from life. Perhaps as much, or even more so, as those rigid individuals who are rigidly devout in their spiritual pursuit. What's there to experience when our senses are numb?

Enjoying life more by experiencing it less seems to be no less than an escape. It means that we cannot handle our fears or our emotions in general. When we're sad, we drink. When we're happy, we drink. When we're anxious, we drink. So, this kind of drunkenness is a rejection of life by an embrace of a mind-altering substance. Getting drunk on life is a pursuit in the opposite direction. Rather than blocking what overwhelms us, we embrace the full spectrum.

When people drink, they often seek to embark on a proverbial rollercoaster ride without fear. They want adventure, they want joyful interactions, they want to encounter someone attractive. And by reducing *fear*, they often experience that it's indeed easier to make these things happen.

Even though fear is uncomfortable, it doesn't mean that it's bad. It means that the body's fight-or-flight response is triggered. So, it's a side-effect of entering unknown territory, which passes when we experience a sense of safety. It's a price we pay to get out of our comfort zone. But the reward is priceless: it's this lucid involvement with elements of life that are new to us; it's the elation of overcoming boundaries and fears.

Being drunk on life means that we are able to fully and consciously enjoy what life, in all its ordinariness, has to offer. And the fact that we seek substances or activities to numb ourselves already indicates that the experience of life is very intense. Sometimes, it seems too intense to handle. And that's where we find the key to getting drunk on life: by riding the waves, no matter how big, while rejoicing when the sea is calm. By not clinging to its highs or lows, but not latching onto its flatness either.

Being drunk on life means embracing it all—not resisting deep sadness and grief when we're dumped or the shivers of fear when facing the unknown, as well as welcoming the tears of joy in a long-awaited reunion, the delight of time spent in nature, the contentment of needing nothing more, and the reverence for life's beauty.

So, how do we get drunk on life? By drinking it.

The paradox is that we can only enjoy life fully when we don't numb the senses as we do when we get drunk. Life itself is already drunk enough. The only thing we have to do is "open up to it," without resistance, with softness, without attaching ourselves too much to our judgments of right and wrong, and transcend the ideas of what we should and shouldn't. Life is simply what is. It's an endless show that we all have a part in. At the end of the day, it doesn't always have to be enjoyed, nor does it always have to be suffered. It simply has to be lived.

Caring Less

A long time ago, Confucius and his students walked on a road to the kingdom of Wei. They stumbled upon a hermit who was at least a hundred years old. The man was gathering some grain that farmers had dropped, and he was singing while doing so. One of the students, a young man named Tzu-Kung, was confused. He couldn't comprehend why the old hermit was so happy, as he must have been *very* poor and alone, having to scour for harvest scraps.

Tzu-Kung walked over to the hermit and showed compassion for his sad fate. But the old man smiled and said: "Why do you feel sorry for me? Am I that pathetic in your eyes?" "Well, sir," Tzu-Kung said, "I assumed you didn't work hard in your younger years and didn't care about success and status. And so, you couldn't find a wife and have children to look after you. You're all alone. How can you laugh and sing?"

"Listen, young man," the hermit said, "I laugh and sing because I feel happy! If I had worked hard in my younger years, competing with others, I wouldn't have gotten so old and healthy. And not having a wife and children? That's great. I don't have to worry about their lives either. It's peaceful. Why shouldn't I laugh and sing?"

This story[16] drawn from the *Liezi* shows a typical Taoist way of thinking, namely, that there's always *gain* in what we perceive as *loss*. Even though the elderly man is not conventionally well-off, he is quite the archetypical "loser" in today's language; he's well aware of his many blessings in disguise. But for most people, it's probably challenging to have this attitude. We're easily swayed by societal standards and concerned with other people's opinions.

This is where Taoist philosophy becomes especially valuable. It contains the wisdom to worry less, not just about what other people think but about *almost anything*. Isn't that something we need today? Just look around—distractions are everywhere, and times are changing rapidly. Life is stressful and demanding, with many suffering from burnout and depression and others on the verge. This chapter shares three insights from ancient Taoist sages to help in caring less in an overly serious world.

1) Not striving for externals

The Taoist sage Zhuangzi observed long ago how people are hung up on things like fame, wealth, and status. In his time, people pursued luxuries, such as expensive food and fine clothes, and traveled to far places to enjoy the sights.

---

[16] You'll find this story in the book *Lieh-Tzu: A Practical Guide to Taoist Living by Eva Wong,* chapter 7: Life is hard work, death is rest

Today, we see nothing has changed. Moreover, our modern-day media constantly pressures us to live a high life. Our tendency to seek out that new, shiny thing, whether luxury or experience, is being exploited.
The more lavish, the better. Society teaches us to have great careers, big houses, nice cars. We get raised under the imperative to be successful and, if possible, wealthy. Material success, status, and achievement are the metrics by which we decide people's worth. It's what the world "honors," argues Zhuangzi. *"If they do not got these things, they are very sorrowful and go on to be troubled with fears,"* he said.[17]

Once you commit yourself to pursuing all these celebrated external things, it seems to be never enough. Once you get a nice car, you will likely want a better one. Once you have your dream house, things get old quickly; the luxury no longer feels that special. The euphoric happiness generated by this once so-much-desired (but pricey) house fades into normalcy. But despite not feeling much happier in the long run, you still have to make your mortgage payments. Over time, you become trapped—a slave to your possessions.

From Zhuangzi's viewpoint, this is a stressful mode of living. People living like this wear themselves out. "This is a stupid way to treat the body,"[18] he stated. And isn't he correct, looking at the rates of burnout, anxiety,

---

[17] *Zhuangzi*, Outer Chapters, Chapter 18: Perfect Enjoyment

[18] *Zhuangzi*, Outer Chapters, Chapter 18: Perfect Enjoyment

and depression in modern-day societies? In pursuit of riches, we *are* wearing ourselves out. In the quest for fame on social media, we're exploiting ourselves. We're doing it because we think it makes us happy. Many do it so other people hold them in high esteem. Others do it to belong, but they're nothing more than cogs in the consumerist machine: a never-ending pursuit of stuff and fame that never satisfies, rarely leading to lasting happiness; something ancient Greek philosopher Epicurus also realized, as he saw many of the things we pursue nowadays as unnecessary and vain.

At the same time, Zhuangzi observed that people look down on poverty, bad reputation, and what we'd call *"irrelevance"* today. Nobody wants to be a nobody. You don't want to be a loser, do you? Losers are the modern-day untouchables. These people don't have the finest clothes, don't eat oysters and caviar, and don't get to see the many fabulous sights of the world. They are to be met with contempt and avoidance.

But Zhuangzi said we can't judge right and wrong by the world's standards. He proposes "doing nothing," as doing nothing leads to perfect enjoyment. "Heaven does nothing, and thence comes its serenity; Earth does nothing, and thence comes its rest," he stated.[19]

We could ask ourselves: Do all these external things truly make us happy? Or can happiness be found in the

---

[19] *Zhuangzi*, Outer Chapters, Chapter 18: Perfect Enjoyment

simplest things? Isn't the mere cessation of trying to pursue happiness when happiness arises? The reason we're unhappy seems to be that we are trying too hard to be happy. And we do so by following a dead-end path. How about we stop striving and let enjoyment unfold?

2) Seeing the positive in the negative

Our achievement society scares us into being useful, self-exploiting members of the capitalist system. We're expected to be good for "something" to participate in the rat race and to be successful in what we do so we can respect ourselves and gain the respect of others.

From the Taoist point of view, we're all playing a silly game. We adopt specific beliefs, mark them as the truth, and act accordingly, taking it all very seriously. Hence, we care greatly about walking in line and what people think about us. People generally fear being disliked and seen as odd, worthless, or inadequate, whatever that means. Most people spend their lives conforming to what society values: having many friends, having a good job, starting a family, and being a useful member of society: "I'm a hard-working, God-fearing, freedom-loving American. And I'm proud of it!" Of course, if you earned your rank in the game, there's no shame in looking down on those we didn't.

But as Zhuangzi said, we can't judge right and wrong by the world's standards. The majority may agree on something, but that doesn't mean it's a universal truth. Taoist sages generally love crushing conventional beliefs. For example, suppose everyone thinks that being 'unambitious' is bad. As Zhuangzi might argue, because of this, people fret greatly about not being seen as unambitious. So, they chase promotions, flaunt their career ambitions, and spend hours discussing their new roles and future plans—just to prove to others that they're driven and worthy of admiration. People who lack such aspirations are generally frowned upon. And for many, that's frightening.

But the Taoist sages challenge us to look beyond societal conditioning. In this case, we could ask ourselves: Is being unambitious truly bad? Is following your ambition really worth the daily stress? What if we choose not to be ambitious—or even refuse to be cogs in the machine? How about we become like the elderly hermit, turning our backs on societal expectations? Would we be worse off or not?

What comes to mind is the story of the useless tree,[20] one of the most profound parables for the way it turns the world upside down in a Taoist fashion.

Carpenter Shih and his apprentice once passed a massive oak standing by the village shrine. The oak's branches could easily shelter hundreds of oxen during

---

[20] *Zhuangzi*, Outer Chapters, Chapter 20: The Mountain Tree

rainfall. Around the oak gathered dozens of people, amazed by its size and beauty.

The apprentice said, "Wow, I've never seen such a beautiful tree. But you don't even care to look at it. Why is that?"

"Are you kidding me?" said the carpenter. "This tree is worthless! Can't you see how crooked it is? Make boats of it, and they'll sink; make closets or doors, and they'll rot instantly! It's useless!"

That night, the carpenter dreamed the crooked tree spoke to him.

"Listen, buddy," the tree said. "I heard you talk. You think I'm worthless, not good for anything. And that's true to an extent. Just look at the apple and orange trees. They're useful. They bring about fruits, which is why people love them. But look at their existence. They're being exploited. When their fruits are ripe, they're subjected to abuse. Their big branches are broken off; they're pulled and jerked around. And when they don't produce anymore, they're cut down. Do you see how their utility makes their lives miserable? They can't even live out the full years Heaven intended for them. I, on the other hand, am of no use. And being useless turned out to be of great use to me. If I had been useful, would I have grown this big? I owe my long life to being useless."[21]

[21] Obviously, this is a personal "contemporary" adaptation of the story

As we see in the story, uselessness, which is generally seen as a bad trait (especially in our achievement society), was a benefit for the tree. It reminds us of the old hermit whose unfortunate life, by societal standards, hid a blessing in disguise. There's always some gain in loss. The trick is to discover it.

3) Finding contentment in what is

Pei-kung-tzu and Hsi-men-tzu, long-separated friends, met again one day. Pei-kung-tzu was astonished at how different their lives turned out. His old friend became wealthy, successful, and respected, but he turned out very poor, and most people didn't like or trust him.

Pei-kung-tzu complained: *"When we both took office in government, you were promoted, and I was dismissed. When we both farmed, even the earth cooperated with you and not with me. When we traded together, you made profits and I lost. This is really unfair!"*[22]

He continued complaining about wearing old clothing, eating food usually given to pigs, living in a broken shack, and being unable to afford a cart. In contrast, his old friend ate the best foods, lived in a giant mansion, and traveled in a luxury vehicle. Didn't they

---

[22] Wong, Eva. *Lieh-tzu: A Taoist Guide to Practical Living (Shambhala Dragon Editions)* (p. 189). Shambhala.

both have the same background and education? Why did their fates deviate so much?

When Pei-kung-tzu confronted his old friend with this perceived unfairness, Hsi-men-tzu exploded, telling him that his success in life stemmed from being more virtuous and, therefore, more worthy in the eyes of others. Of course, Pei-kung-tzu felt depressed after this slap in the face and sought consolation from the village sage. The sage visited Hsi-men-tzu and asked him why he insulted his friend. Hsi-men-tzu promptly explained that Pei-kung-tzu simply couldn't stand that he was less worthy than himself. However, the sage corrected Hsi-men-tzu, explaining that worthiness cannot be measured by social or political success. He simply had more luck in life.

You are successful in society not because you are particularly wise or virtuous but because you have luck in everything you do. On the other hand, Pei-kung-tzu's failure to be recognized is not due to stupidity or lack of virtue. It's because he does not have luck in everything he does.[23]

When Pei-kung-tzu heard what the sage said to his old friend, he felt better about his situation. He no longer let his lack of luck be a reason for unhappiness.

---

[23] Wong, Eva. *Lieh-tzu: A Taoist Guide to Practical Living (Shambhala Dragon Editions)* (p. 190). Shambhala.

The story shows us that embracing fate and finding contentment, whether rich or poor, successful or not, leads to inner peace. We often can't do much about how things work out around us, but we can control our attitudes toward these things. Usually, our best bet is to let things go their natural course and focus on how we navigate through them instead of trying to control them.

Is there a more relaxing attitude in a fast-paced, stressful world than letting all these attachments and must-haves slide and take life however it comes? Who's more successful? The wealthy person waking up dissatisfied every morning, always chasing more? Or the poor person, waking up content, happy with whatever the Heavens give him?

Loser

Is it truly bad to be a loser? As mentioned in the introduction, the ancient Taoist sages loved to mock social conventions, seeing them as hypocritical and often hindering true fulfillment and happiness. For example, many in today's society consider chasing wealth and fame to be good and ambition to be admirable. But are these ideas objective truth? Or, as the Taoists would argue, are these just man-made concepts that do more harm than good? The Taoist sages urged people to reject social conventions that cause harm and misery, even if it meant being judged as a "loser" in today's terms.

Yang-chu, for example, a philosopher who appears[24] in the *Liezi* text, explained that attaining wealth or reputation is futile. Sure, both can be beneficial. For instance, wealth generally leads to more opportunities for pleasure, and a good reputation may open doors that usually remain closed. However, there are no guarantees. And, in many cases, chasing wealth and reputation costs us more than it provides in return, as it's a stressful ordeal. Just imagine the energy it takes to amass resources or the uphill fight trying to maintain a good reputation, which is predominantly out of your control, as people's opinions are as fickle as the wind. Moreover, according to Yang-

---

[24] You'll find this story in the book *Lieh-Tzu: A Practical Guide to Taoist Living* by Eva Wong, chapter 72: A name is nothing and titles are empty

Chu, we destroy ourselves in our attempts to climb the social ladder at the expense of happiness.

In today's hustle culture, chasing "success" is like a religious duty. People push each other to achieve, often at the cost of their well-being, leading to stress, anxiety, and burnout. Society glorifies "winners" and treats "losers" as pariahs, almost as if *not* achieving is a moral failing. But is this fair? Is being a "loser" really so bad?

We've discussed the concept of the modern-day loser several times already. This chapter sheds light on it through the lens of Taoist philosophy. We'll be looking at the *Liezi* text, specifically the creative translation by Taoist scholar Eva Wong, which, in my opinion, has some interesting perspectives regarding this topic.

1) The modern-day loser

So, what does it mean to be a loser these days? Dictionaries have countless definitions of the word "loser." First and foremost, a "loser" means someone who "loses," such as losing a game. However, the term is also currently used as a derogatory term to indicate someone who is unsuccessful or even unattractive. It's not just someone who failed at a particular pursuit; it has become a societal archetype characterized by failure, not living up to expectations of success and achievement. Being a loser seems to have more weight than just "having failed." It's like having done something terrible; it's almost as if *not* being ambitious in today's achievement-oriented society is a form of blasphemy.

A Dutch article from 2023 tells the story of Joost and Iris, two unrelated people who claim not to be ambitious. Joost argues that his attitude has led to stigmatization. He feels that if you're labeled an unambitious person, you're someone who refuses to reach his full potential and keeps himself small in a world of unlimited possibilities. Iris feels that not being ambitious is a curse word these days, and thus, she often feels guilty for her *lack* of ambition. The article also features author Marian Donner, who argues: "The Western world is so focused on becoming the best version of yourself. It always has to be more and better, in every aspect."[25]

Ambition is a great virtue these days. For many, it's an important, almost obligatory factor in being attractive dating material. And "just doing your job" is often not what employers want to hear; they want someone willing to grow and self-improve constantly, on top of their job. Striking is the apparent hostility toward people who don't conform to the cult of ambition. Perhaps that's why a derogatory word for people who don't achieve much exists. It's almost as if you're committing a crime by not pursuing your ambitions.

---

[25] Joost (28) heeft geen ambities: "Ik word gestigmatiseerd in deze prestatiemaatschappij," NPO, 20 June 2023

The meaning of good and evil has changed throughout the ages, evolving based on factors like society, religion, and culture. In the past, in a Christian context, for example, being good meant being virtuous, and being bad meant being sinful. But, in today's society, have success and failure become the new virtue and vice? Have losers become the new sinners? In other words, are you a bad person if you're not ambitious and aren't achieving?

Considering current societal values, such as "becoming the best version of yourself" and "always improving" or, as philosopher Byung-Chul Han puts it, constant "self-optimization," refusing to engage in these things goes against the grain. When achieving is "good," not doing so (or not aiming to do so) is, so it seems, "bad": an attitude that people like Joost and Iris experienced firsthand.

Moreover, many seem to believe that a person's lack of success is their fault; they just didn't work hard enough. They just didn't put in the effort to succeed. If they would have only worked harder, they would have made it, just like that small minority who did. There's this collective belief that everyone can succeed if they work hard for it. But is that true? And even if it's true, is there anything wrong with people like Joost and Iris choosing not to be ambitious? And if so, why then?

The Taoist sages described in the *Liezi* text have different views on the matter. According to them, pursuing material success is a waste of time, and judging people based on their achievements is a big mistake.

2) The limitations of effort

In the story *"Effort argues with Destiny,"*[26] Effort and Destiny appear as characters discussing who's more influential: *Effort* or *Destiny*. Effort claims that his achievements are better than Destiny's, but Destiny takes this into question. As a counterargument, Destiny recalls countless examples that show that neither effort nor talent decides people's trajectories. For instance, he noted corrupt officials who are rich, honest, excellent workers who are poor, talented, virtuous people who remain unknown, and the untalented who rise to the top. Destiny continued, saying: *"If you are as effective as you say, then why don't you make the hard-working people rich? Why don't you give virtuous people a long and prosperous life? Why are the intelligent and able people not employed, and why do stupid people occupy important places in government?"*[27]

The story reminds me of being a content creator on YouTube and the ongoing discussion about whether success (or a lack of it) depends mainly on a creator's

---

[26] You'll find this story in the book *Lieh-Tzu: A Practical Guide to Taoist Living* by Eva Wong, chapter 62: Effort argues with Destiny
[27] Wong, Eva. *Lieh-tzu: A Taoist Guide to Practical Living (Shambhala Dragon Editions)* (p. 188). Shambhala.

effort or the algorithm. Many argue that success on the platform is almost entirely in your own hands; you just have to make good videos and create great titles and thumbnails, and you'll *get there*. And some claim everyone can do this as long as they work hard. For these people, *success boils down to effort.*

Moreover, if you happen to *fail* on YouTube, well, it's your fault. Blaming the algorithm or other factors outside yourself isn't fair; it's all on you or, at least, for the most part. Many channels follow advice from so-called experts. They create good content and craft compelling thumbnails and titles like their successful peers. Yet, they remain invisible, disproving the experts' claims. At the same time, saying "Hawk Tuah"[28] during a street interview lands someone in a partnership with Jake Paul and makes that person's podcast one of the most watched in the world.

In our achievement-driven society, we overestimate the power of effort and the amount of control we have over our success, as if succeeding depends almost entirely on hard work. Survivorship bias is an essential factor in such reasoning. Sure, some indeed make it, but does that mean everyone will? Does that deny the role of destiny in their success?

---

[28] Referring to a short-lived internet sensation called the "Hawk Tuah girl" (Haliey Welch), whose career ended after being involved in a cryptocurrency controversy.

From the Taoist perspective, you cannot flat-out *deny* the role of destiny. Luck and chance are always deciding factors. Not everyone is blessed with high intelligence, creative talent, a stimulating environment, good mentors, et cetera. We don't get to choose the cards we're dealt with. Thus, many we consider "losers" may simply have been *unlucky*; they may have suffered factors beyond their control that significantly shaped their fate.

3) Fortune and worth

As mentioned earlier, an achievement-driven society values ambition, success, accomplishment, and, in many cases, material wealth and fame. If you have all of those, you've made it. You're considered a successful person. A loser, however, lacks these things. A loser, therefore, is seen as someone less worthy, someone of lower value. The unfortunate term "low-value male" has become common lately, describing an unsuccessful man who is unattractive because of his lack of success; it's someone you don't want to be, someone worthy of contempt.

The idea that material success, fame, or achievement equates to worth is strong and widespread. However, from a Taoist viewpoint, it's also a social construct. It's not an objective truth. It's simply what people have agreed upon. The term "loser" has no real meaning; it's just a label based on society's focus on shallow measures of success.

Unfortunately, society's emphasis on success and achievement is considerable, causing people to suffer. But why do we place so much importance on success and failure? And aren't we wasting our lives being concerned with this dichotomy?

4) Success and failure

Despite societal ideals, the Taoist sages believed that anticipating success and failure was a waste of time. Moreover, the *Liezi* dedicates a chapter to why these concepts are not worth chasing, as doing so only causes anxiety.

The chapter *"Success and Failure"*[29] doubles down on the observation that success and failure are largely out of our control. We never know beforehand if we'll succeed or fail. We can work ourselves into an early grave; a desired outcome is never guaranteed. Yet, in pursuit of it, we may exploit ourselves for years, chasing success and wealth, until we break down, leaving irreparable damage to our bodies and minds. We'll be anxious, obsessed with succeeding, constantly worrying about the future.

But gaining success *itself* isn't the problem. Achievement isn't bad. What's bad is the relentless striving toward it, the *attachment* to a desired outcome.

---

[29] You'll find this story in the book *Lieh-Tzu: A Practical Guide to Taoist Living* by Eva Wong, chapter 69: Success and failure

According to the *Liezi*, we're better off accepting the role of destiny:

Only those who accept the natural flow of events will not be concerned about life and death or anxious about praise or blame. Intelligent people will often want to calculate the likelihood of success and failure before they take action. However, their chances of succeeding are often not very different from those of people who do not think about the odds.[30]

5) The real losers

Despite human influence, things will happen as they happen. Some people won't succeed, no matter how hard they try. Others succeed without doing much for it. This just goes to show how relative being a "loser" is. Destiny decides we can't all be winners, no matter how hard we strive for it. So, why put so much emphasis on achieving an ideal that is ultimately not in our control?

But suppose we let go of the attachment to success and failure, seeing it for the capricious phenomena they are. In that case, the derogatory term "loser" is rendered meaningless—it loses its weight. Sure, we'll still be losers in the view of others. They may see us as failures, lazy,

---

[30] Wong, Eva. *Lieh-tzu: A Taoist Guide to Practical Living (Shambhala Dragon Editions)* (p. 208). Shambhala.

unmotivated, et cetera. But according to the Taoist sages, that's not something to be concerned about as reputation is also among the things ultimately not up to us.

The Taoists, however, don't say you shouldn't pursue anything or give things your best shot or that you should neglect yourself. The *Liezi* posits that although chasing riches can injure you, poverty can also hurt you. But clinging to outcomes causes suffering. The *Liezi*'s viewpoint is this: *People who manage to accept destiny and detach from outcomes will be calm and at peace in the face of adversity.*

Moreover, and this is my own addition, being okay with being a "loser" means letting go of the fear of failure and the fear of not conforming to societal ideals—fears that may be stopping you from truly being yourself.

The Art of Not Trying

Not Trying

Those who stand on tiptoes do not stand firmly.
Those who rush ahead don't get very far.
Those who try to outshine others dim their own light.

Laozi, *Tao Te Ching*, chapter 24

How can we improve when we stop trying to improve? Many people waste their efforts trying to better their lives with questionable results. They gain knowledge and chase external things while exhausting their bodies and burdening their minds—only to end up discontent.

The Taoists observed that humans tend to act in ways that are counterproductive. And in their attempts to alter the natural way, they only make things worse. All these strivings, rules, ethics, and values are surely invented to benefit humanity. But according to the ancient Taoist sages, we should get rid of them all. Why? Because all these manmade ideas only remove us further from the natural flow of life.

Trying to alter what nature has intended is like swimming against the stream: it's exhausting and gets us nowhere. Behind the ever-changing universe lies a mysterious and undefinable force that the Taoists call "Tao," for the lack of a better word. The "Tao" is all-encompassing, and it's beyond anything that our senses can perceive. We cannot intellectually comprehend it, yet many have tried.

Humans tend to conceptualize things that are beyond their understanding. They use names and categories, and they select and discern, but they fail to grasp what the universe is truly like. Instead, they create deceptions, artifices that make life understandable for humans. But by trying to comprehend, they lose the Tao.

1) The tragedy of trying

"Five colors blind the eye. Five notes deafen the ear. Five flavors make the palate go stale," wrote Laozi.[31] So, by arranging colors, notes, and flavors, we might enhance our understanding, but we also limit it, as there's so much more outside of these fixed concepts. The same goes for the human tendency to make rock-solid rules for everything to get a sense of control. Again, we limit ourselves by doing so because the world is ever-changing, and what works today may not work tomorrow.

Also, from a sense of solidarity and justice, people create immense bodies of ethics, moral codes, and rituals that form an artificial way of life. Even though the intentions are good, they try to make things work while building their own prisons. Now, let's talk about the word "trying."

I think most of us are familiar with the idea that we should simply "act" and not "try." This idea is closely

---

[31] Laozi, *Tao Te Ching,* chapter 12

related to the "flow state." In a "flow state," one becomes the act, like a dancer who becomes the dance or the poet who becomes the poem. This is wu wei, a concept that can be literally translated as "non-doing" or "doing nothing." In the context of the flow state, wu wei translates best as "effortless action" because we act in a smooth and painless manner.

In the context of this chapter, however, translating wu wei as "non-doing" or "doing nothing" fits best. Literally, "doing nothing" is often seen as unproductive and as a useless way of being, in which there's no progression. But according to the Taoists, nothing is further from the truth. When we keep in mind that the universe is in flux and in a state of entropy, we'll realize that there's always progression in the natural flow of life. So, instead of using force and exhausting ourselves (which is the favorite method of today's culture), we could travel through life much more easily by using intelligence. Because isn't it so that so many times, problems seem to solve themselves? And that by "taking action," we often make things worse?

When we waste our time trying to improve things, we distance ourselves from the natural course. We repeatedly act in ways that are (according to the Taoists) unnatural and waste our bodies and minds doing so. So, why do we do this?

It probably has a lot to do with how we attribute value to certain things. For example, when we're averse to poverty but desire money and fame, and when we're averse to being lonely but desire to be part of something. So, we try to eradicate the former and increase the latter, while the latter cannot exist without the former. Also, we think that it's necessary to conform and alter nature based on certain belief systems. We try to better the world, while the results of our interventions are kind of questionable.

2) How we try

Now, how can we bring these ancient theories into the modern world? According to Taoist thinking, in what ways do we, modern humans, often "try," but our efforts only leave us with peanuts in the end? Let's explore some examples of how we "try" using the ancient Taoist scriptures, the *Tao Te Ching* and the *Zhuangzi*. The first one is: *Trying to improve the world.*

Alan Watts, fervent scholar of Taoism, once pointed out that the goodie-goodies of society are the biggest troublemakers. Their "must-save-the-world" attitude often disrupts the natural course simply because they seek to enforce man-made ideas of what's good and evil. In the *Zhuangzi*, we find a story[32] about a man named Yen Hui, who asked Confucius for permission to travel to the country of Wei after he heard that it was ruled by an incompetent ruler. Yen Hui wanted to use everything he

---

[32] *Zhuangzi*, Inner Chapters, Chapter 4: In the world of men

had learned about governance to improve the country of Wei.

Confucius, however, discouraged him from doing so. Not only because Wei's highly disagreeable leader probably wouldn't listen but also because people, in general, don't like outsiders coming in and telling them what's better for them from a place of moral supremacy. As Confucius stated: *"If you do not understand men's minds, but instead appear before a tyrant and force him to listen to sermons on benevolence and righteousness, measures and standards—this is simply using other men's bad points to parade your own excellence."*[33]

We could ask ourselves: In what way is using other people's faults to create a nice role for ourselves a genuine virtue? That's probably why so-called "social justice warriors" are so hated. We won't improve a situation by one-sidedly demonizing groups while placing ourselves on the moral high ground. This only creates more division, more tension, and makes it even more unlikely that changing things for the better in a sustainable manner is possible. As Laozi puts it in the *Tao Te Ching*:

Do you want to rule the world and control it?
I don't think it can ever be done.
The world is a sacred vessel and it cannot be controlled.

[33] *Zhuangzi*, Inner Chapters, Chapter 4: In the world of men

You will only make it worse if you try.
It may slip through your fingers and disappear.

Laozi, *Tao Te Ching*, chapter 29

The second one is: *Trying to be happy.*

No matter if it's the pursuit of money, status, fame, power, or knowledge, these ongoing efforts to be happy are the reason why we aren't. We think that we'll be happy when we've got a million dollars in the bank, or when we have finally published that book, or when our YouTube channel has 100k subscribers, but this is hardly the case. Sure, we enjoy some momentary pleasure, but that's not happiness, according to the Taoists. Moreover, in this pursuit, we exhaust our bodies and minds while, tragically, never achieving what we're looking for.

This is what the world honors: wealth, eminence, long life, a good name. This is what the world finds happiness in: a life of ease, rich food, fine clothes, beautiful sights, sweet sounds. This is what it looks down on: poverty, meanness, early death, a bad name. This is what it finds bitter: a life that knows no rest, a mouth that gets no rich food, no fine clothes for the body, no beautiful sights for the eye, no sweet sounds for the ear.

People who can't get these things fret a great deal and are afraid—this is a stupid way to treat the body. People who are rich wear themselves out rushing around on business, piling up more wealth than they could ever use—this is a superficial way to treat the body.[34]

When chasing happiness is a blind alley, what should we do instead? Well, the Taoists give us some suggestions. But before we go into them, let's look at the third one: *Trying to be something else.*

The *Zhuangzi* tells us a story about animals and the wind that envy each other for their inborn characteristics. The centipede envies the snake for the fact that it can move without legs, but the snake envies the wind for its ability to travel great distances without having a body at all. However, the wind argues that it takes just a finger or foot to hinder it.

All in all, nature has created everything with its own attributes. Nothing is better than the other; only judgment makes it so. Thus, we feel the need to change who we are just to fit some societal ideal. Also, we try to change ourselves because we want to conform to a manmade standard, *to fit in,* simply because we're seen as *defects* when we don't. So, a sixth finger is cut off just to comply with the five-finger standard.

Why can't we just be who we are, the way *nature* intended us to be? That would be so much easier. Everyone and everything has its place in the whole. And by trying to alter this, we bring the world into disbalance.

---

[34] *Zhuangzi*, Outer Chapters, Chapter 18: Perfect Happiness

When people see things as beautiful,
ugliness is created.
When people see things as good,
evil is created.

Being and non-being produce each other.
Difficult and easy complement each other.
Long and short define each other.
High and low oppose each other.
Fore and aft follow each other.

Laozi, *Tao Te Ching*, chapter 2

How can we put these ideas into practice? The Taoists suggest several things. First of all, the *Zhuangzi* points to the benefits of taking the middle path. This means that we shouldn't stretch ourselves beyond our means but rather stay centered so we conserve our health and stay close to our own nature:

Follow the middle; go by what is constant, and you can stay in one piece, keep yourself alive, look after your parents, and live out your years.[35]

The Tao is constant. And one who seeks the Tao unlearns something new every day, according to Laozi.

---

[35] *Zhuangzi*, Inner Chapters, Chapter 3: The secret of caring for life

So, instead of limiting ourselves to a belief system, we let go, keep an open mind, and give the universe room to show itself as it is. Trying to change nature is a futile pursuit, as is trying to blur our vision of nature with man-made constructs.

Instead of adding to knowledge, we let go of knowledge until we reach a point of inner stillness. Only then do we open ourselves up to the Tao, or what we, from a theistic point of view, could call God. In this state of emptiness, we feel content. And contentment is true happiness. The Taoists call this process the "fasting of the heart" (see chapter "Fasting of the Heart"). By unlearning something every day, the Taoist arrives at non-action. It's the art of not trying while nothing will be left undone.

Winning

Competitions can be nerve-wracking. The closer we get to the day on which we are supposed to shine, the more anxiety builds up. What if I perform badly? What if something goes wrong? An Olympic swimmer trains thousands of hours just to get that medal. A musician practices for days on end just to perform well those few times on stage. And a student practices a speech in front of the mirror multiple times just for that moment in front of the audience. When all their efforts come down to *one* defining moment, how can they *not* succumb to the pressure of the need to succeed?

Zhuangzi was a keen observer of nature, including human nature. He figured out that the burden of the future often negatively affects our performance in the present moment. To illustrate this, he tells us a simile about an archer.

When you're an archer, and you shoot simply for fun, you shoot with skill. But if you shoot for a small prize, you begin to worry about your aim. And if you're competing for gold, you become a nervous wreck.[36]

Zhuangzi tells us that our skills, thus the competency of doing a certain task, are the same in all three situations. But, somehow, we let different circumstances influence

---

[36] *Zhuangzi*, Outer Chapters, Chapter 19: Mastering Life

our skills in different ways. Let's analyze this story to show how this works.

When we play for fun, winning or losing doesn't matter. This means that we aren't burdened by possible consequences. When we shoot some balls simply to have a good time, missing the goal doesn't mean much, as we're not competing. Practicing a speech in front of the mirror by ourselves does not come with the risk of damaging our reputation because there is no audience.

When there's nothing on the line, there's nothing to be anxious about, meaning that there's no fear that sabotages our performance. When burdens like "trying to win in a conceptual future" or "trying to prevent repeating a horrible failure from the past" are absent, we are more immersed in the act itself. That's why, in many cases, the best speeches are given in front of the mirror, the best soccer goals are made on the practice field, and the best musical performances are done outside the studio and far away from the stage.

But suddenly, there are consequences tied to your performance. By performing well, you might be able to obtain a medal or even a championship trophy. And within the game of human civilization, these aren't just meaningless objects. These prizes represent symbols of success that come with an increase in reputation and, in some cases, an opportunity to monetize our success. Winning could lead to becoming rich and famous. Losing, however, could result in falling out of people's favor, shame, guilt, the end of a career, and losing the chance of gaining money. So, there's a lot at stake. Because of this, a desire for winning arises, along with an aversion to losing, until we conclude that losing is no option.

Feeling the necessity to win has a positive side: it motivates us to practice a lot and make sacrifices. Thus, necessity is a breeding ground for success. However, necessity can also become a burden that sabotages our performance. In the case of the archer, the prospect of winning and losing made him a nervous wreck. With the possibility of winning gold also came the possibility of "not having it" or "having blown the chance of winning it." His thoughts about a potential loss produce fear and, thus, ruin his chances.

When we're too focused on winning and losing, then our worries overshadow our skills. Our skill is still the same, but the mind creates a fog of thoughts that prevent our skill from unfolding. In such situations, we find ourselves not being in "the zone." We might even start to believe that we've lost our "mojo." But this isn't the case: it's our mind sabotaging itself. When our thoughts about the past and future fall away, our skills can manifest optimally to the point that we become "one with the act." A great example of this is a dog catching a ball.

When the dog sees you throwing the ball, it jumps toward it with great precision and catches it without even thinking about landing, as it's focused purely on catching the ball. It doesn't act because of a prize. It acts for the sake of acting. Catching a ball is part of the dog's nature. However, we are not dogs. We're humans. Our nature is different. We can plan for the future in detail, and our goals are generally much more sophisticated. We're often expected to perform our best with a future goal in mind.

But even then, we can still influence what we focus on. Do we let the possibility of winning a gold medal dominate our thoughts? Or do we let this desire fade into the background and focus on what we can do at this very moment? The less we care about the results, the less our minds will be troubled by them. This applies very much to creative work as well.

When creating just for fun, it's an easy process. But when we're obsessed with getting views, outperforming other channels, and judging our creations as failures and successes, we feel more pressure. The need for success, the desire for fame, and the prospect of getting paid can overshadow the overall performance of a content creator. Thus, when there's something on the line, in some cases one's livelihood, then what once was a joyful pastime *has the potential* to become a stressful and anxiety-provoking chore.

Worrying about the results obstructs our ability to focus on the task at hand. This is detrimental, as our best performances are the ones that we're immersed in. This immersion is known as the "flow state." In this state, a swimmer forgets the water, a soccer player becomes the field, and a painter becomes one with the movement of her brush. Within that moment, they don't try to *win* anything and don't act for the sake of *obtaining a prize*; they have switched off their expectations and desires and reduced their very "being" to the act. And that's key. Just do it.

Not Doing

Have you ever reflected on the word "doing"? "Doing" points to performance, achievement, and effort. It also implies that there's a "doer" who engages in "doing something," and that there's a passive element or "the thing that's being done." But does it work that way? Is there a separation between the thing that "does" and the thing that's "being done"? Or is the thing that does actually what's being done and vice versa?

The sages might urge us to think about "doing" (and "not doing") a bit differently than we're used to. From the Taoist viewpoint, everything happens as a whole, meaning that activities that seem isolated, individual, and independent are part of one big cosmic dance. This means that when we stop "doing," from a human perspective at least, the universe (including ourselves) is still moving on.

The Tao is the natural flow of existence, where things are not forced or controlled but allowed to unfold. This means that it's not entirely clear who or what is the doer, and who or what is being done. Things just happen, so it seems. The flow of existence is something we allow or resist. If we follow the Tao, our lives will be easy. But if we try to resist, our lives will be difficult.

When we're mainly focused on striving and straining, convinced that only through "effort" will we get where we need to be, we may be swimming against the stream. So, what if "doing" isn't always necessary to get things done? What if many of our actions are a waste of time and energy? What if we can take shortcuts in life, if we learn how to embark on the natural course?

1) Are we doing or being done?

From a Taoist viewpoint, everything operates together, as the world is a sequence of components without a governing center. Sure, we could argue that the governing center of the body is the mind. But the mind is also governed by its environment. Without the environment, there's no mind. But without the mind (and senses), there's no environment, as there's nothing to perceive it. When we observe how the world operates, we discover that everything is interdependent. There can only be high when there's low, light when there's dark, front when there's back. Or as philosopher Alan Watts stated, *"There are no bees where there are no flowers, and there are no flowers where there are no bees."*

The relationship between humans and the environment is similar. Even though we think we're separate from our surroundings, we still need a ground to stand on, food to eat, and oxygen to breathe. If we take a look at our breath, for example, we'll see that we have a choice: when we're conscious of it, we can control the breath, but for the most part, the breath "happens" to us. We can't live without the breath, and the breath can't exist without us. So, who's the doer, and who's being done?

This system of interdependence is the reason that nothing can arise without an equal opposite. These opposites continuously move around a center, attracting and repelling, influencing and being influenced, merging, separating, being part of one big organism; one big happening. And this system, always in motion, is the flow of the universe, or Tao.

In this grand manifestation, we're as much human as we're the universe. Is a drop of water in the ocean a drop, or is it the ocean? When the ocean forms waves, is it the drops of water that make up the waves, or is it the ocean as a whole?

As human beings, we're part of and subject to the greatness of the universe, but we are also the universe. And the universe has a way of its own. Like a river, it flows at its own pace. Knowing the Tao, therefore, means becoming aware of the flow of life. And once that happens, we can flow with it effortlessly and let life carry us instead of us carrying life. However, this is not what most people do.

2) Resisting the flow of nature

Force is followed by loss of strength.
This is not the way of the Tao.
That which goes against the Tao
comes to an early end.

Laozi, *Tao Te Ching*, chapter 30

The Tao represents natural order. It doesn't force but allows everything to fall into place. But this rather passive and accepting stance is not endorsed in our culture. We are encouraged to always be striving, always be acting, never be idle, and not to wait for things to happen but to make things happen.

We seem to believe that progress and change are products of action only and that if we let nature run its course, everything falls apart. But this collective pathological need for control leads to us building sandcastles in the surf. We fight uphill battles, sail off against the wind, and exhaust ourselves doing so.

We can fight aging, for example, as much as we might want to by undergoing surgery or by using special anti-aging creams and hair dye; no one has ever escaped the decay of our bodies, aside from those who died young. Like apples, we grow, and then we break down and die. How much energy do we spend fighting this inevitable part of life? How much strength can we save by not seeing aging as such a big deal and allowing for change to occur?

The same goes for time. What's gone is gone; what's ahead lies ahead. We can hold on to a rock, unable to let go of times that lie in the past. By doing so, we don't see what's unfolding to us in the present, as we're only interested in preserving what cannot be preserved, which is the past. In this case, we're doing, but nothing is getting done.

The problem with going against the flow of life is that we're part of it anyway. No matter how tightly we grab a rock or a branch, no matter how fiercely we swim against the stream, the river still carries us in a certain direction, whether we like it or not. It's unavoidable.

Nevertheless, waging war against the flow of life is considered the normal thing to do. For some reason, always choosing the path of most resistance deserves respect, even when the results are questionable. But what's normal isn't always good, and what's good isn't always normal. Sometimes, it's better not to follow the herd, especially if the herd's behavior gets us nowhere. So, what can we do instead?

3) Doing without doing

Being and non-being produce each other.
Difficult and easy complement each other.
Long and short define each other.
High and low oppose each other.
Fore and aft follow each other.

Therefore the Master
can act without doing anything
and teach without saying a word.

Things come her way
and she does not stop them;
things leave and she lets them go.

Laozi, *Tao Te Ching*, chapter 2

The essence of doing without doing is getting things done without taking action or without effort. Doing nothing means that we let nature do its work as much as possible. We don't control but delegate. We don't force but allow.

The more we allow things, the more order we will have, as the flow of nature is the order in itself, and disorder appears by our interventions. If we're too busy grasping, we aren't open to the things coming our way. When a fisherman is impatient, he'll only scare the fish away, but when he's patient, the fish might come to him.

Doing without doing is the way of the shortcut. "The easy way," as Alan Watts put it. It's the art of using any situation to our advantage. There are ways to accomplish this. It all starts with achieving a state of 'stillness," in which we observe and let the dust settle so we make room for the world to unfold. Instead of trying to figure things out (which often leads to overthinking), we relax and let the insights arise naturally.

By being still, it's also easier to adapt to the current situation, as we're in a state of observance. Adaptation and flexibility are key if we want the easy way because every set of circumstances has its advantages, threats, and opportunities.

When you can't leave the house, for example, the easy way is to focus on tasks you can do inside and around the house. And when you're in traffic in another country, instead of trying to control and impose your will on this alien situation, the easy way is to go with the flow and "be led" instead of leading.

But it's also a matter of figuring out the course of the water current so we can get a free ride, so to speak. The sailor who's aware of the wind can use it to his advantage. And people who manage to ride the wave can make a lot of money quickly and easily. That's why people seek to capitalize on trends or even crises, as they can function as a tailwind.

Thus, it's also the art of getting the best results with the least energy possible. However, I think it's important to note that the "easy way" isn't always the "good way" when it comes to ethics.

Doing without doing means that we become receptive to nature's ways so they can flow through us and carry us where nature wants us to be. Like drunkards, we become soft, loosen up, let go of our inhibitions, lower our guards, give up resistance, and just let things play out.

In a way, it's how we fall asleep. We can't force ourselves to fall asleep, but we make it happen, preferably in the right circumstances. This is also the case with creativity. We can't *force* creativity, but we can create the circumstances in which the creative flow is more likely to occur.

Doing without doing requires trust. Trust that, despite our *inaction*, "change" will happen, as change is nature's default. And the more we cease to work against it, the more we allow the universe to take care of itself. Or as Laozi stated: "When you arrive at non-action, nothing will be left undone."[37]

---

[37] Laozi, *Tao Te Ching*, chapter 48

Fasting of the Heart

In psychology, as well as popular culture, we've seen the emergence of different types of detox. The dopamine detox, for example, also called the "dopamine fast," is currently presented as a way to "reset" our brain's reward system by abstaining from all kinds of activities that bring pleasure. This serves different purposes. One of them is increasing our motivation, as our brain learns that pleasure isn't so easily available anymore, so it becomes more willing to make an effort to obtain it. Another purpose is working with our addictions, as abstaining for a period of time weakens the relationship we have with things we're addicted to, so the problem becomes easier to handle. The method of *Alcoholics Anonymous* is based on abstinence, for example.

The idea of detoxing ourselves from outside influences isn't new. The ancient Taoists acknowledged the value of letting our minds rest so we stop the exhausting maelstrom of judging, identifying, analyzing, fantasizing, et cetera. According to the Taoists, silencing our faculties for a while not only replenishes our energy but also brings us closer to "Tao."

The "fasting of the heart" entails a temporary abstinence from intellectual as well as sensual activity. This concept isn't just about detoxing the mind; it's about detoxing the soul by shutting down the mind and the senses.

The term "fasting of the heart" was coined[38] in the *Zhuangzi*, in which Confucius had a conversation with one of his pupils, Yen Hui. Yen Hui wanted to travel to the kingdom of Wei and bring about change by using his knowledge and wisdom. Confucius criticized Yen Hui's plans for being a bit too "ego-driven," as no one is waiting for a know-it-all who enters the kingdom and starts telling people how to live.

When Yen Hui asked what he should do then, Confucius advised him to start fasting. Yen Hui then replied: "My family is poor, and for many months we have tasted neither wine nor flesh. Is not that fasting?"

"The fasting of religious observance it is," answered Confucius, "but not the fasting of the heart."

For a Westerner, the heart has a different meaning than for a Chinese person. The word "heart," in this context, is translated from the Chinese word "Xin" (心), which could be translated as "mind" because the ancient Chinese believed that the heart was the center of human cognition. Thus, the "fasting of the heart" is actually the "fasting of the mind." Confucius explained it by saying that it "cultivates unity" by curbing the senses and the workings of the mind. Or as he states: "You hear not with the ears, but with the mind; not with the mind, but with your soul."

[38] *Zhuangzi*, Inner Chapters, Chapter 4: In the world of men

Because our mind cannot know the Tao, and our five senses cannot perceive it, the only way to get closer to the Tao is by stopping the mind and senses, so there's nothing left to disturb the connection we have with it. So, it's a subtractive process, a way of letting go in order to unite with the Tao and experience oneness with the universe. So, it's the abundance of thought and sensory activity that prevents our soul from what Confucius called "cultivating unity."

Even if the idea of Tao doesn't appeal to us, we can still benefit from the fasting of the heart, as it's an ultimate detox of everything that disturbs our being (or should we say our non-being). This helps us to achieve what so many people try to achieve through sensual pleasure: inner peace, or just simply: a break.

The senses are the gateways between the world around us and our minds, as we think about what the senses pick up. The mind is a powerful tool, but it can also be an immense burden, especially when it's out of control. The mind's survival mechanism is based on making distinctions. Good and bad, beautiful and ugly, healthy and unhealthy, et cetera. But in the Taoist worldview, these are just modulations of opposites that are inseparable. In other words: there is no high without low, there is no good without bad, there is no beauty without ugliness, and so forth.

Seeing the world in opposites also creates friction. Our fears, our aversions, our hatred, and all the actions that follow are products of our discerning faculties. It's the old story of us versus them, which also serves as the basis for the perceived separation between humans and nature. Needless to say, this mechanism serves an important purpose, too. Without it, how can we distinguish friend from foe? Or a good decision from a bad one? Without thinking, how can we plan for the future and learn from the past?

Using the mind helps us to thrive, communicate, achieve goals, protect ourselves, and stay out of trouble. But when we let the mind use *us*, there's a chance that it becomes a liability rather than an asset. The more we attach ourselves to our beliefs, the more hostile we become to different views. The sterner we are, the more brittle we become. The stronger we desire something, the more painful not acquiring the object of our desire will be. The more troubled our thoughts, the darker we see the world. The more we feel that we possess something or someone, the more fearful and domineering we become.

The continuous chatter of the mind exhausts itself as well as the body. How can we find inner peace when we're constantly plagued by thoughts? "Cultivating unity," therefore, is the liberation from the clash of opposites and the experience of the interconnectedness of everything, which can be achieved by quieting the mind.

Can you coax your mind from its wandering
and keep to the original oneness?

Can you let your body become as supple
as a newborn child's?
Can you cleanse your inner vision
until you see nothing but the light?
Can you love people and lead them
without imposing your will?
Can you deal with the most vital matters
by letting events take their course?
Can you step back from your own mind
and thus understand all things?

Laozi, *Tao Te Ching*, chapter 10 (Stephen Mitchell)

When our hearts fast, we become passive and receptive. When we become still like a pond in the center of a valley, the mud settles, and the water becomes clear. When we let things slide and don't intervene, the universe takes care of itself. Confucius probably knew that the fasting of the heart would show Yen Hui that it was better not to intervene and let the kingdom of Wei figure out their own course. His mingling with a business not his own would probably have made things worse.

As Laozi stated: "For those who practice not-doing, everything will fall into place."[39] And so, it works with the mind. Could it be that all our neuroses, addictions, and compulsive engagements with pleasurable activities are products of the mind's tyrannical efforts to intervene with

[39] Laozi, *Tao Te Ching*, chapter 3

the world and with itself? Do we embark on a "dopamine detox" because we can't bear the tormentors in our heads any longer? If so, then abstaining from external pleasure may only take us so far; the solution to our problem lies in our hearts.

Wu wei

Once upon a time, a novice farmer indulged himself in motivational videos. He became familiar with ideas like the importance of "effort," the "hustle culture," and "work hard, play hard." After binge-watching for days, he walked onto his farm, fired up and determined to make it a great success. He started by pulling up one of the crops as a way to make them grow faster. But this didn't work. Then he began to water the plants twice as much, hoping to make them grow faster, but he drowned them instead. After trying to force his success, the farmer realized that no matter how much effort he put in, acting in opposition to nature is counterproductive.

Despite humanity's technological developments and will to progress, we're still utterly dependent on nature. Human effort has its limitations and is always in conjunction *with* nature. We cannot grow a plant, for example, completely isolated from natural growth, even though we can influence and manipulate it.

In the *Tao Te Ching*, Laozi explains that the world governs itself. It doesn't need our intervention. As Laozi wrote: "When you arrive at non-action, nothing will be left undone."[40] This idea resembles the basic understanding of the paradoxical concept of "wu wei." But when we look for a definition of wu wei, we quickly

---

[40] Laozi, *Tao Te Ching*, chapter 48

discover that there isn't one fixed meaning. Some translate wu wei as "non-action" or "doing nothing," others as "actionless action," and still others as "effortless action."

We find out that Taoism offers several layers, if you will, regarding how wu wei can enhance our relationship with the world. And how this ancient art of "letting things happen" doesn't necessarily make us passive, ignorant bystanders but can actually improve how we act, leading to better outcomes.

1) Wrestling with nature

Probably the most common interpretation of wu wei is quite literally aligning our actions with nature without forcing anything, acting only when it's suitable. Laozi stated that using force always leads to unseen troubles. With force, he doesn't seem to point to the literal use of force per se but rather to "forcing the flow of nature." Nature has its course. It's always working in the background. It lies at the root of humanity's existence and continually creates and recreates what the Taoists call the 10,000 things: everything under heaven and beyond.

But despite the immense propulsion of the universe, today's society places the importance of conscious human effort above all. We *celebrate* effort, regardless of its actual effectiveness, as we aim to always be busy for the sake of being busy. As modern Sisyphuses, we push rocks uphill just for the sake of pushing.

Making an effort is one thing, but *intelligently* making an effort is another. Yes, sometimes hard work is necessary, and action is appropriate, but on many occasions, it isn't. It depends on the rhythm of the game, on the cards you're dealt, and whether or not it's your turn. Acting out of turn means going against the flow of the game.

Hence, we often experience that "forcing things" leads to ruin in the long run and that pushing our luck beyond nature's constraints backfires. On the other hand, situations often solve themselves when we *don't* force or intervene. By letting things happen, things get done naturally.

The novice farmer, for example, simply needed to leave his crops alone and be *patient*, and nature would do the rest. But when it's time to reap, the farmer should roll up his sleeves. "The Tao never acts with force, yet there is nothing that it cannot do,"[41] Laozi stated. If we'd just go along with nature, then everything runs smoothly. The farmer's task is to sow the seeds, the seeds' task is to grow into crops, and then the farmer's task is to reap the harvests when they're ready. This is how nature works optimally.

---

[41] Laozi, *Tao Te Ching*, chapter 37

Laozi believed that the world cannot be governed, as the world governs itself. It's entirely out of control. Trying to control it is always a losing battle. And spending our lives fighting against nature is a waste of time, no matter how much people celebrate us for engaging in such a heroic endeavor. Instead of spending our life energy trying to control, govern, and change the natural course of things, we're better off accepting what *is* and navigating through it like water flowing over a rocky surface toward the ocean.

Some are meant to lead,
and others are meant to follow;
Some must always strain,
and others have an easy time;
Some are naturally big and strong,
and others will always be small;
Some will be protected and nurtured,
and others will meet with destruction.

The Master accepts things as they are,
and out of compassion avoids extravagance,
excess and the extremes.

Laozi, *Tao Te Ching*, chapter 29

2) Acting for the act itself

When we go deeper into the meaning of wu wei, it becomes even more intriguing.

With effortless action, we could say that we're not so much "doing" as "going." We embark on a river stream without considering where it brings us: we're setting sail into uncharted territory, but don't let the great unknown faze us. We swim along with the current, not against it, making our way smooth, devoid of stammers and hiccups. Swimming against the current takes effort; so does holding tightly onto a rock. When we force things, problems arise.

Does this sound vague? Let's consider an example: going on a date. The person you're going to meet is interested in one thing only: getting to know *you*, the person you are at that moment. But many people overprepare, overanalyze, and rehearse what they're going to say. And so, the nerves come in; people overcompensate, are disingenuous, and come across as staged.

Why is this the case? Most likely because we focus too much on the results. Zhuangzi talks about how different prospects can influence our actions and emotional states if we attach ourselves to them. The chapter *"Winning"* explains this in more detail, using Zhuangzi's parable of the archer.

In the context of a date, most of us want the date to become a success; we want the other person to like us. So, there's pressure involved; there's a price to be won, and if we don't get it, we feel miserable. And thus, what could have been a fun, joyful night out becomes a strenuous, forced, stressful event, with lots of discursive thoughts and mental preparations in advance. We are standing in our own way, blocking the natural flow of the universe, which we cannot possibly control, no matter how much thought and planning we throw at it.

But imagine that you enter a date utterly unprepared, without even seeing it coming. Now, you're acting naturally and are living in the moment because the spontaneity of the event means you haven't had the opportunity to overthink. There has been no time for planning, plotting, or analyzing, and all that remains is the pure you: present and one with the moment. And most people love that. So, if we manage to let go of the results, we can act more effortlessly and responsively, just for the act itself.

3) The uncarved block

If we go even deeper, we arrive at the ego and emptiness. Because of past experiences, social conditioning, or ideologies, we have molded ourselves into knowledgeable, cultured human beings that fit the context they're in. This context could be a religious community, a country, or a profession. We generally see this as a good thing. But there's a downside. And this downside has to do with the ego.

The ego often distorts how we perceive the reality of the world. When we approach a situation, for example, a conversation with a spouse, the ego tends to fill in the unknown gaps with all kinds of prejudices, fantasies, and convictions. The larger the ego, the more it will dominate the situation, subsequently closing us off from what's truly going on. Therefore, people with strong convictions experience great difficulty seeing the world in another light—or outside the confines of their intellectual prison.

Hence, Laozi urges us to return to a more unprocessed state, which he calls "the uncarved block." We could see the uncarved block as a person who is unencumbered by all kinds of intellectual baggage, which allows his vision of the world to be clear.

Dr. Woei-Lien Chong, a Dutch philosopher and sinologist, explains her interpretation of wu wei in a Dutch book about Taoist philosophy, emphasizing the element of emptiness or "openness." She describes the essence of practicing wu wei as follows:

> *And so the whole practitioner is able to, from the clarity of his egoless center, observe all relevant forces in a certain situation in their being, undistorted, so he can respond to them flawlessly.*[42]

---

[42] Woei-Lien Chong, *Inleiding taoïstische filosofie*. Handelen vanuit het innerlijke centrum, p. 110 (quote translated by Einzelgänger)

If we look at wu wei this way, it's not just letting go, going along with the flow of nature, and allowing the universe to do its job: it's a *much bolder* move for which we need a lot of courage. We have to be brave enough to let go of what we've learned, throw our normative frameworks in the trash, and flush our assumptions through the toilet. Or as Laozi put it:

Renounce knowledge and your problems will end.
What is the difference between yes and no?
What is the difference between good and evil?
Must you fear what others fear?
Nonsense, look how far you have missed the mark!

Laozi, *Tao Te Ching*, chapter 20

Zhuangzi tells us a story about a conversation between Confucius and one of his pupils, Yen Hui. Yen Hui wanted to travel to the kingdom of Wei after he heard about its many problems and tyrannical ruler. So, he planned to use his knowledge and wisdom to lecture the king of Wei and steer the kingdom in the right direction.

Confucius persuaded Yen Hui not to do it, telling him that his plans were too ego-driven and wouldn't work. After all, no one is waiting for a know-it-all coming out of nowhere, telling you how to take care of your business, let alone a self-absorbed tyrant. But still, Confucius offered an alternative, which he called the "fasting of the heart."

Confucius described the "fasting of the heart" as a form of meditation, which leads to letting our preconceptions go and making room to receive. With an open and receptive attitude, Yen Hui would learn about Wei and its king, their customs and beliefs, the situation as it plays out, and eventually be much more capable of lending a helping hand. In this understanding of wu wei, we let go of the ego, so we act in accordance with the situation at hand as it is.

We let things happen and act responsively, unrestrained by our limited, preconceived ideas. Or as Laozi points out, we return to being uncarved blocks. As Dr. Woei-Lien Chong stated:

No matter if it's about politics, governance, diplomacy, or any other activity: What Zhuangzi calls wu wei is this ultimate receptive and responsive way of action, from a crystal-clear openness in yourself, one with the breathing of the cosmos.[43]

---

[43] Woei-Lien Chong, *Inleiding taoïstische filosofie.* Handelen vanuit het innerlijke centrum, p. 110 (quote translated by Einzelgänger)

Flow

We often hear of remarkable people who, through dedication and practice, seem to become one with their craft. An example of such a person is Tsao-fu, a character from Taoist literature[44] who wished to become a skilled charioteer. So, he seized the opportunity to apprentice under an expert widely known for his exceptional mastery. Years passed, and Tsao-fu served his master without receiving *any* instruction or lesson; he just worked and followed commands. But rather than becoming disheartened, he displayed commitment, convincing the charioteer that he was worthy of his teachings.

One day, the master finally offered him a lesson. But it wasn't what Tsao-fu expected. Instead of jumping straight into charioteering, the master put a couple of wooden posts into the ground and had Tsao-fu jump from one post to another repeatedly. After much practice, he could glide effortlessly across the wooden posts. And so, the master revealed the essence of the practice: it wasn't just about strength or skill but about the union of *intention* and *action*. With the reins, hands, body, and mind in harmony, the chariot felt like an extension of Tsao-fu himself. The action was effortless as he found himself in a *flow state*. The master stated:

---

[44] You'll find this story in the book *Lieh-Tzu: A Practical Guide to Taoist Living* by Eva Wong, chapter 60: *Tsao-fu learned to drive*

When your mind is clear and your body is relaxed, you can control six bridles without confusion, and twenty-four hooves will step where you want them. Then the wheels of your chariot will move forward and in reverse, and turn left and right with precision and control. You can drive on mountain roads with the same ease as you would on the plains. Your driving will not be different whether your horses are stepping close to the edge of a cliff or running on flat grassland. That is all I have to teach, so remember it well![45]

The flow state, or "being in the zone," is a mysterious thing. It's an optimal state of performance, an idea our minds are fond of but, ironically, aren't able to create at will. We can't will ourselves into the flow state. On the contrary: the more you force it, the less likely you'll get into it. And the more frustrated you become by not reaching it, the further it gets out of reach until you're so done with trying that you give up entirely and focus on something else. But precisely in those moments, it appears like a fish approaching the fisherman's hook, just after he gave up trying. The flow state is unreachable but not out of reach. You can't grasp it. It grasps you. But only if you let it.

---

[45] Lieh-tzu, *A Taoist Guide to Practical Living* (Eva Wong), *Tsao-fu learned to drive*

This chapter focuses on the psychological dimension of flow. What's happening in our brains when we're in the flow state? What does academic research say about it? Why is it so elusive? And, perhaps most interestingly, what can we do to *achieve* it?

1) When I stopped trying

Let's begin with a personal story. As far back as I can remember, I've been an overthinker and over-analyzer. I've spent a significant portion of my life in my head, analyzing, daydreaming, and contemplating the past and future, *not* paying attention to the present moment. Now, I only recently learned how to drive a car, which was probably one of the most challenging things I ever had to learn. My driving instructor told me that my "thinking" is my greatest enemy when learning this skill: I overthink and analyze *a lot*, which interferes with my driving. After much practice, I finally got my license.

As I've been driving for a while now, I noticed that when I'm too much in my head, I get a bit anxious when it's busy on the road, and I drive more nervously. But then, all of a sudden, it's like I'm one with my car, the road, and the surrounding traffic, as if the crowded highway is one giant organism I'm part of. In those moments, I experience the flow state.

When contemplating the flow state when driving, I immediately think about a recent trip with my mom and sister to the Ardennes, a forest region in Belgium and Luxembourg that extends into France and Germany, with hills, ridges, and rivers, only a few hours away from the flatlands I come from. When you're used to everything being as flat as a pancake, because that's what it is like across most of the Netherlands, driving in the hills is a slightly different ballgame. The first thing I noticed is that my car responds differently to going up a mountain compared to descending one, which is the *most basic* physics.

However, for some reason, it startled the Dutch operating system in my brain, which has *no* software installed to deal with elevations in its environment. This was my baptism of fire. My first time driving abroad on a different terrain. At the beginning of the trip, I felt slightly anxious. I was about to expand my comfort zone. I tried to plan, analyze, and sort out all possible scenarios in my head. I wanted to impress my mother and sister with my driving skills. I was a bit worried about the Belgian roads, which are notoriously bad, and about not understanding the traffic rules of our Southern neighbors.

So, I was driving and driving, passing the city of Eindhoven, crossing the Limburg province, toward the border when dark clouds, thunder, and lightning began to appear all around us. It was raining cats, dogs, Democrats, Republicans, and Eurosceptics. I could barely see the driver before me, let alone check what was happening a hundred meters ahead. My baptism of fire became a baptism of lousy weather and a ridiculously chaotic highway. I remember how that moment pushed me into the present. I had no choice other than to ignore all discursive thoughts and drive. I stopped trying to drive well and just drove well without even intending to drive well. This sounds paradoxical because it is. When my desire to drive well ceased, I actually began to drive well. What started as this overanalyzing galore of desperation became an effortless and unexpectedly delightful experience.

Mountain sights and curling highways came and went; cars and trucks overtook me, and I overtook them as if we were bees, a swarm sharing a common conscience, almost as if something greater than ourselves diligently orchestrated the spectacle of traffic driving between Liège and Namur. Oh, and the Belgian roads were pretty good, especially in the Ardennes. What baffled me was how euphoric it all felt. Just being there, one with the highway, the traffic, the car. And the deeper I fell into this state, the more that anxiety became something alien, something far away, unable to touch me.

Looking back on my experience, I couldn't believe that it went so well. It was weird, considering how dangerous driving is, to have felt as comfortable behind the wheel as sitting on the couch watching Netflix while continually paying attention to the highly unpredictable and fast-changing. But any attempt to analyze and sort out what constituted my effortless driving and how I did it didn't generate any satisfying answers.

I remember my driving instructor saying before my exam, "You can drive now. You've learned everything you need to do so." It's a simple statement but profound. When we practice something well and for long enough, the things we learn reside within us; they become part of us. Most of the time, it's not a matter of consciously applying what we've learned. It's more about removing the intellectual blockages and getting out of our own way, so to speak, to allow these abilities to arise.

The flow state is elusive, an enigma of the mind or, perhaps, from *beyond* the mind. Yet, there have been people who attempted to unveil its mysteries, to find out how it works and what triggers it. So, how *does* it work? The remainder of this chapter touches upon research and literature, exploring the psychology behind the flow state and how we can provoke it.

2) The psychology behind "flow"

One of the leading experts on the flow state is Mihaly Csikszentmihalyi, a psychologist *and* university professor who wrote the best-selling book *Flow*. In his book, Mihaly reveals that what makes an experience "genuinely satisfying" is "a state of consciousness called *flow*." Mihaly defines the flow state as being engaged in an activity that is both challenging to one's skill level and intrinsically rewarding. In the flow state, we tend to experience intense and focused concentration on the present moment, loss of reflective self-consciousness, a merging of action and awareness, and even an altered sense of time. It's what constitutes an optimal experience, as he describes in his book:

It is what the sailor holding a tight course feels when the wind whips through her hair, when the boat lunges through the waves like a colt—sails, hull, wind, and sea humming a harmony that vibrates in the sailor's veins. It is what a painter feels when the colors on the canvas begin to set up a magnetic tension with each other, and a new thing, a living form, takes shape in front of the astonished creator.[46]

Mihaly also noticed that such events of optimal experience do not depend on external circumstances. People in horrible conditions, such as imprisonment in concentration camps, have reported these optimal experiences, or flow states, as well. In fact, according to Mihaly, the flow state occurs when someone voluntarily stretches his body or mind to its limits to accomplish something difficult and worthwhile. So, these moments aren't necessarily pleasurable or comfortable. Consider

---

[46] Csikszentmihalyi, Mihaly. *Flow: The Psychology of Optimal Experience* (Harper Perennial Modern Classics) (p. 3). HarperCollins.

running a marathon or being at the height of a battle in a computer game, wholly immersed in it; these moments take a toll on one's body and mind yet embody the optimal experience or flow state.

But we often hijack the flow state through what Mihaly calls "*psychic entropy*," a state of inner disorder and chaos in the mind; it's the opposite of the flow state. Instead of being focused, our attention is scattered; instead of operating in the present moment, we're all over the place, be it lingering in the past or worrying about the future. Instead of action and awareness being merged, they're apart from each other, separated by an information overload. In a state of psychic entropy, generally, *not* much gets done, and *what* gets done goes less than smoothly. As Mihaly stated:

> *Whenever information disrupts consciousness by threatening its goals we have a condition of inner disorder, or psychic entropy, a disorganization of the self that impairs its effectiveness. Prolonged experiences of this kind can weaken the self to the point that it is no longer able to invest attention and pursue its goals.*[47]

Psychic entropy can have different causes. There could be too many distractions; for example, you're

---

[47] Csikszentmihalyi, Mihaly. *Flow: The Psychology of Optimal Experience* (Harper Perennial Modern Classics) (p. 37). HarperCollins.

working on an essay while your WhatsApp web application runs in the same browser, and Instagram messages are coming in while listening to a podcast with the television on in the background. These are constant interruptions of information that create a sense of chaos in the mind. Similarly, multitasking can also cause psychic entropy, as doing too many things at once scatters one's attention. Another cause is interpersonal conflict, as it generally occupies the mind: we tend to repeat arguments and imagine confrontations, which takes our focus away from engaging in constructive and enjoyable tasks.

Whatever the cause is, it always comes down to excessive information flooding one's consciousness. A prevalent example of this is worrying. When we worry, we try to impose order onto chaos and the unknown—the moments before I drove to the Ardennes, worrying about the unfamiliar terrain, Belgian traffic rules, impressing my mom and sister, and the weather conditions caused my psychic entropy. Essentially, I only had one task: driving from point A to point B. But a stream of information overflowing my mind interfered with that one task, leading to anxiety and scattered attention. And amid the psychic entropy behind the wheel, I tried hard to drive well, forcing that smooth and effortless experience on the road, something that initially didn't happen, causing me frustration, which added another layer to my psychic entropy.

All this "trying" to drive as well as possible through analysis ironically led to paralysis. I was standing in my own way. The action was taking place on the road. However, my awareness was taking place in my thoughts. Something needed to happen, some kind of sudden awakening, some sort of proverbial slap needed to happen to shock me out of my head into the midst of action. The satisfying challenge of navigating my car through the storm and the unfamiliar Belgian roads did that pretty well.

3) The mystery of flow

The problem with the flow state is that it's impossible to force it; you can't *will* yourself into a flow state using effort. It's as if the more we try to be in a flow state, the less likely we are to enter it. Only when we stop trying to conceptualize the flow state or trying to use our intellect to attain it will it grasp us by surprise without us even realizing it. So, it seems, as from my driving experiences, it's not something to attain but rather something to allow. But does that make the flow state something entirely unattainable: a random experience that may occur when we're lucky?

According to Mihaly, the emergence of the flow state isn't entirely random. He noticed that there are conditions for the optimal experience or flow state. The conditions become apparent when we engage in what he calls "flow activities," such as sports, rituals, art, and, I'd say, gaming as well. These activities are designed to make flow experiences easier to achieve, according to Mihaly, as they facilitate the conditions that trigger the flow state. Flow activities have rules and clear goals to attain, and they provide immediate feedback. We have a sense of control over these activities and can track our progress. However, all flow activities have one thing in common: a transformation of the self takes place by making it more complex. By "complex," Mihaly means the development of skills, experiences, and knowledge, an example of which is mastering rock climbing or painting. Flow happens when such transformation takes place.

When engaging in a flow activity, Mihaly distinguishes two non-optimal states: *anxiety* and *boredom*. Anxiety occurs when one's skill level is too low for the activity in question. Boredom occurs when the activity is too easy for one's skill level. Hence, there's hardly any fun in playing *Age of Empires 4* against a complete noob as a Gold-rank player (which is an average skill level). So, the match will very likely be a boring one: no transformation takes place, as there's no challenge and no opportunity for growth. But playing against a level 2 Conqueror isn't fun either because there's such a discrepancy in regard to "skill level" that the average player doesn't stand a chance.

When the activity means just being repeatedly obliterated by a vastly superior opponent, a flow state won't likely occur. Therefore, playing against players of around the same skill level (preferably slightly above) is optimal. However, when one's skill increases, it's important to keep playing with matching opponents to prevent boredom. So, there should be a balance between challenge and skill level.

A caveat is that the experience of challenges, competition, and progress is subjective; some people need more "challenge" than others, and different people experience the flow state in different activities. My sister, for example, finds her flow state during rock climbing but not in writing essays, which is where I experience it. So, for a significant part, where one's flow state lies is personal.

Thus, it seems the flow state isn't so mysterious; it's actually quite logical: it's a consequence of certain conditions, just as a meal is the consequence of a recipe. The flow state while driving was a fortunate coincidence of external and internal ingredients. Now, the question remains: What can we consciously do to achieve the flow state?

4) Achieving flow

When the poet becomes the poem, the driver the drive, and the painter the painting, that's the flow state. It's when trying has ceased and the conscious desire for optimal performance or outcome has waned. It's when the mind has stopped telling you what if, why, when, and even how. It's when, as the mythical Cook Ting stated in the *Zhuangzi* when effortlessly cutting up oxen: *"Perception and understanding have come to a stop and spirit moves where it wants."*[48]

It happens when you stop trying. Crave for it painfully, and it will elude you. Forget about it and simply enjoy what you're doing, and it appears. There's no direct way of catching it. But when the conditions are right, it may appear. So, how can we create these conditions?

Here are some practical tips derived from Mihaly's work: Do something you enjoy, find your challenge-skill balance, set clear goals, make sure you get immediate feedback, focus on the task at hand, and thus, let go of planning, worrying, or ruminating about the past or the future; go all the way into whatever you're doing.

When it comes to the focus part, there are several things we can do to enhance that, such as engaging in mindfulness and meditation practices. Rituals and warm-up routines can help, too: they make the mind ready to engage in the task, which becomes more effective when they become habitual and when they include an activity that reduces discursive thinking.

Near the end of his book, Mihaly says that the forms of psychic entropy that currently invade the mind and cause us so much anguish are likely to have been recent

---

[48] *Zhuangzi*, Inner Chapters, Chapter 3: The secret of caring for life

invaders of the mind. They're products of a vastly increased complexity in society, culture, and our minds. In simpler times, humans were closer to animals in terms of flow; there was the occasional psychic entropy in times of danger, hunger, or pain, but overall, we were free from the worries brought about by the complex societies of today. Is there a way back to such a simple mode of existing? It would be very difficult (and almost impossible) to operate in today's world. Thus, the challenge we face is to return to what is, in essence, a more *primordial*, harmonious mind state in the face of our highly complex, modern environment.

Solitude, therefore, can help achieve flow, according to Mihaly. I mean, let's face it. Solitude allows us to turn away from the world, at least for a while, especially if we disconnect from certain media outlets. The constant flow of information, the noise of catastrophizing media, the warped showcasing of people's lives, and the consumeristic ideals of what you should own and do with your time are significant birthplaces of distraction. Hence, for some activities and some individuals, solitude is essential.

The Power of Softness

Softness

The rigid and stiff will be broken.
The soft and yielding will overcome.

Laozi, *Tao Te Ching*, chapter 76

Generally, people admire “strength” and look down on “weakness.” We associate strength with being firm and energetic. Strength allows us to accomplish things, fight back against adversity, not be swayed by the world around us, and be assertive. It gets us places; we find it attractive and praiseworthy, and thus, many aspire to be unbreakable pillars of strength. We see the praise of strength all around us: we praise muscular bodies, wealthy entrepreneurs showing off their mansions and car collections, and political leaders who use strong language and don’t shy away from using military action.

Weakness, on the other hand, we tend to associate with impotence, incompetence, fragility, being pushed around easily, and being powerless. Weakness gets us nowhere; we find it unappealing and try to avoid it. In fact, we often hide our weaknesses because we’re ashamed of them.

But there’s more to weakness than it generally gets credit for. Despite all of the negative connotations, weakness, at its core, means a lack of strength, which is not necessarily a lack of power. Strength implies being hard and firm; weakness implies being soft and malleable. But being soft and malleable is far from impotent.

Furthermore, softness (and, therefore, weakness) has the power to overcome strength if used in the right ways. "Weakness is how the Tao works," wrote Taoist sage Laozi. Strength isn't always the answer. In many situations, softness, not strength, weakness, not firmness, is the way to go, and we're better off yielding than fighting, adapting than opposing, submitting than dominating.

1) The king and the philosopher

Once upon a time, there was a king who only hired strong and brave men, believing that these men were the most capable of protecting him. Then, a philosopher paid a visit. He told the king that a better strategy would be one that leads to people not even daring to strike him in the first place. The king agreed. But then, the philosopher argued that despite fear, people could still wish to harm the king, which isn't ideal. So, he said, a better strategy would be one that would make people not want to harm him at all. The king nodded. Then the philosopher said:

But just because people do not want to harm you doesn't mean they will respect you or love you. Suppose you had a strategy that could get them to love you and respect you, so that your concerns are their concerns.

Would this strategy be several times better than just strength and courage?[49]

The king became very enthusiastic when the philosopher suggested that he rule with virtue and integrity. He had his military force, anyway. So, by being good to the people, he'd become loved and respected rather than feared, and his popularity would surpass that of many sages.

In such a position, the king most likely wouldn't need to hire strong men to defend him with force because very few people would desire to strike him. Compare this to the leader who rules using intimidation and fear. Even though he might succeed in protecting himself and his position as a leader, he'll attract constant opposition. People will hate him and try to strike him, so he needs to increase his strength to protect himself. And so, he's stuck in a vicious cycle. Such leaders quickly get isolated and far removed from their people because they *oppose* and *oppress* the people instead of aligning with them. It's a very exhausting and unsustainable position.

Governments ruled by tyrants are rarely durable; they eventually get destroyed from the inside out. Not without reason, Laozi wrote that the worst leader is the one who is despised. A good leader, on the other hand,

---

[49] Wong, Eva. *Lieh-tzu: A Taoist Guide to Practical Living (Shambhala Dragon Editions)* (p. 96). Shambhala.

puts the people's interests first and is loved by the people. The best leader is hardly visible.

The power of softness wins here. Brute strength may get one so far, but the soft approach may result in not even needing such strength. The power of softness focuses on prevention, carefully creating circumstances that reduce the likelihood of problems happening instead of focusing on fighting problems that could have been prevented. Laozi stated:

Take care of difficult problems
while they are still easy;
Do easy things
before they become too hard.

Laozi, *Tao Te Ching*, chapter 63

2) Taming the tigers

An animal caretaker named Liang had a way with wild animals like tigers and wolves: he knew how to tame them.[50] In fact, he made them so tame that he could let them roam around in his courtyard. Liang took an apprentice to pass on his expertise and explained that the secret to taming these animals was understanding their

[50] You'll find this story in the book *Lieh-Tzu: A Practical Guide to Taoist Living* by Eva Wong, chapter 17: The art of taming tigers

nature. One should not force their will on them nor try to rouse their ferocity.

The key to success lies in caution and adaptation. For example, the caretaker would not feed live animals to tigers, as this would arouse their ferocity. He would not feed them when they were hungry or full, so they'd be contented when fed. *"If they get too happy or excited, they may become angry. You need to keep them in a balanced state, not too happy, and not discontented,"*[51] said the caretaker.

By doing so, the tigers felt comfortable roaming around in the caretaker's gardens. Liang didn't use force. He adapted his approach to the animal's nature, carefully deciding his actions, and it worked. If he had forced his way, the tigers would probably have retaliated or left. The soft approach is the intelligent approach. It doesn't come from a place of anger, impatience, or fear but *wisdom*.

Take, for example, the enormous prison population in the United States. A significant body of research suggests that locking people up does more harm than good. It does not help people to improve their outlook; it does not facilitate successful integration into society. It's a harsh and blunt method of dealing with criminals based on anger and fear rather than wisdom.

---

[51] Wong, Eva. *Lieh-tzu: A Taoist Guide to Practical Living (Shambhala Dragon Editions)* (p. 78). Shambhala.

Finland, on the other hand, has open prisons. These facilities have no locks and gates, and the prisoners wear no uniforms and go into the city to shop for groceries. The inmates are allowed to work, study, and care for themselves. They learn self-control, as opposed to regular prisons where *everything* is controlled. Instead of spending their sentences in detrimental conditions that only worsen their outlook, the prisoners are stimulated to improve themselves, which prepares them for successful reintegration into society. Despite criticism of this soft approach, the system works, as the reoffending rate of these prisoners is one of the lowest in the world. Here, again, we see the power of softness. In the case of crime, the gentle approach deals with the root of the problem, not just the consequences.

The root of the problem is often complex and could be linked to a difficult childhood, poverty, demographics, lack of opportunity, lack of education, or just sheer misfortune in life. It thus asks for a delicate approach, one that fits the individual. Instead of locking these people up, the soft method is to try and help them in such ways that they don't desire to engage in criminal activity in the first place.

3) Soft overcomes the hard

Laozi described the power of what he called the softest and most yielding substance: *water*. As soon as you touch it, it moves. If you blow over it, water will bend with the air. It's also easily mixed with other substances and, therefore, easily polluted. It never retains form by itself, as it always needs its surroundings to shape it. When you obstruct it, it changes course. It simply adapts and settles when you capture it and put it in a pool. When it's hot, it evaporates. When it's cold, it freezes. It doesn't want to accomplish anything; often, it's just doing nothing. It doesn't reside in higher places but naturally seeks the lowest.

In many ways, water is weak. Yet, as stated at the beginning of this chapter, people generally like strength and look down upon weakness. We don't want to yield; we push back. We don't want to be flexible; we stand our ground. We don't want to give in and submit; we defend our positions and dominate. We don't want to be soft and bending; we act hard and firm. In contrast, the ancient Taoists believed that softness isn't inferior to strength. Moreover, they asserted that softness could overpower the hard and strong, as is the case with water.

Water is the softest and most yielding substance.
Yet nothing is better than water,
for overcoming the hard and rigid,
because nothing can compete with it.
Everyone knows that the soft and yielding
overcomes the rigid and hard,
but few can put this knowledge into practice.

Laozi, *Tao Te Ching*, chapter 78

Imagine a room with a group of men discussing a specific subject. Some of these men have little knowledge about the issue yet dominate the conversation. Others have some knowledge about the subject and use that to fight back against the nonsense uttered by those with little knowledge. Then there's one man with the most knowledge about the subject who only listens and asks questions. Who's the smartest guy in the room?

It's the one with the most knowledge, not just because he's the most knowledgeable, but also because by positioning himself in the lowest position, he gains more knowledge and new insights on top of what he already has. Instead of using strength to dominate the conversation and impose his knowledge and ideas on others, he uses the "soft" approach of humility and receptivity by listening and asking questions. He's willing to update his expertise if possible.

Through his gentle approach, he overcomes the "rigid and hard." By seeking the lowest position, he resides in the most unpopular yet most fertile place: the place where the water flows to.

4) The rigid and stiff

The living are soft and yielding;
the dead are rigid and stiff.

Living plants are flexible and tender;
the dead are brittle and dry.
Those who are stiff and rigid are the disciples of death.
Those who are soft and yielding are the disciples of life.

Laozi, *Tao Te Ching*, chapter 76

Being firm in one's principles is often considered a positive characteristic. Firmness helps us survive. By being firm, we protect ourselves against deception, create order out of chaos, and create clarity out of ambiguity. We don't fall for anything by standing for something. But if we're too firm, we become rigid, stiff, inflexible, and thus unable to adapt to circumstances that might ask us to update our fundamental ideas. Soon, the world becomes uninhabitable for us because we've become incompatible with it. We're cut off from life as dead pieces of wood amid a blooming forest.

Change is life, and life is change. When we're flexible, we easily go along with an ever-changing reality and, thus, are more in tune with life. Survival of the fittest doesn't mean survival of the strongest but of those that best manage to "fit" and "adapt" to their circumstances. So even though survival requires strength, it also needs the softness of adaptability. You either adapt or perish. Or as Laozi stated: *"The rigid and stiff will be broken. The soft and yielding will overcome."*[52]

---

[52] Laozi, *Tao Te Ching*, chapter 76

Be Like Water

Water is the softest and most yielding substance.
Yet nothing is better than water,
for overcoming the hard and rigid
because nothing can compete with it.

Laozi, *Tao Te Ching*, chapter 78

Many people are hijacked by the rigidity of their minds. Thinking in categories and fixed ideas can be a great crutch for survival, as it creates clarity in a chaotic universe. But thinking too rigidly also has its negative consequences. Seeing the world in categories and separate boxes limits our perception, so we become stuck in our ideas of how things are or are supposed to be.

As the universe is ever-changing, and most things, if not everything, are more complex than our minds can comprehend, a more fruitful approach to life would be one that is flexible and tangible, one that enables us to flow along. You know . . . a bit like *water*.

Laozi celebrates flexibility. He opposes the rigid life stance that some people choose to take. In contrast to what many think, weakness, or more specifically, the ability and willingness to yield, can actually be a great strength, according to Taoist philosophy. Hence, Laozi states that the supreme good is like water.

One thing that characterizes Taoist philosophy is a deference toward nature. The ways of nature are all-encompassing. The dance between opposites is the fundamental principle of how the universe works, which manifests as ongoing change. When we observe nature closely and through a Taoist lens, we can see two forces at work: yin and yang, or the feminine and the masculine.

Yang consists of the more active elements of existence, like speed, restlessness, productivity, excitement, aggressiveness, and being outgoing, as well as hardness, dryness, and stiffness. Yin consists of the more passive elements, like silence, receptiveness, and not reacting as opposed to reacting, as well as softness and flexibility.

Our culture celebrates the *yang* aspects of life. It's all about faster, bigger, more, better, standing your ground, defending your unchanging opinions, confronting and clashing with the enemy, and altering rather than adapting.

Yin aspects, on the other hand, are looked down upon. For example, being receptive to opposing opinions and being willing to change your views is often seen as weak. "If you stand for nothing, you'll fall for anything," former American politician Alexander Hamilton famously quoted, which may be true, but if we're not willing to maintain certain flexibility, never change our viewpoints on anything, never change our approach, and are never willing to bend with the winds of life, we become as rigid as a dead branch.

1) Increased resilience to change

When we observe the nature of water, we discover that it's extremely resilient to change, as water is able to take all kinds of different forms. We can pour water in a glass, and it becomes the glass; when it's part of the ocean, it blends in with the waves; and as a river, it flows. Depending on its temperature, water changes its behavior: when it's cooked, it evaporates, and when it's frozen, it becomes solid. Thus, water survives many different circumstances by adaptation.

The softness of water adds strength to living beings because it makes them flexible and, therefore, more resilient to outside circumstances. As Laozi stated:

The living are soft and yielding;
the dead are rigid and stiff.
Living plants are flexible and tender;
the dead are brittle and dry.

Laozi, *Tao Te Ching*, chapter 76

Things that are brittle and dry will break easily and are either dead or equivalent to being dead. The same goes for minds that are rigid and stern. People who are rigid and stern generally have difficulties dealing with change, as they desire permanence rather than the uncertainty of impermanence.

Unfortunately for these people, change is inevitable. Life *is* impermanence. If life were permanent, it would be lifeless. Thus, when we don't accept the reality of impermanence, we waste a lot of energy fighting the inevitable. Change in life comes in different forms. For example, we can experience small changes, such as having a new colleague. Or we can experience big changes like moving to another country, going through a divorce, or even facing death.

Now, if we compare life to a river, we can see its subtle twists and turns as small changes; a drastic change in course would represent a big change, and when it discharges into the ocean, it would symbolize death. We see that, no matter what happens, the river flows along with the changes in circumstances, adapting to different landscapes and finding its way past obstructions without effort. Even when faced with its inevitable annihilation, the river approaches it without being troubled, without resistance, as it simply merges into something else.

Thus, we live life in a continuous flow, finding our way around everything that crosses our path, not resisting even the most drastic of changes, including death. But also, when we are contained like water being kept in a jar, we still and *become one with* the jar until our circumstances change.

2) The power of softness

Laozi argues that the soft overcomes the hard. He takes water as a metaphor for this assertion; water is soft and flexible, but it also has the power to erode even the hardest materials like rock and metal.

Everyone knows that the soft and yielding
overcomes the rigid and hard,
but few can put this knowledge into practice.

Laozi, *Tao Te Ching*, chapter 78

To be like water, we need to know *how* we can overcome the hard by being soft. "Not forcing" anything is central to Taoist philosophy. In practice, we can see that using *force* is not only exhausting, but it often doesn't get us anywhere. Now, this doesn't mean that we should *never* use force in certain situations. But in many cases, the soft approach is superior to using force when it comes to long-term results, as well as saving our energy and maintaining a tranquil mind.

This mechanism is best explained through examples. A great example of the power of softness can be found in the movie *The Shawshank Redemption* (based on a novel by Stephen King), in which the protagonist, Andy Dufresne, is sentenced to life in Shawshank State Penitentiary for murdering his wife and her lover, even though he keeps saying that he didn't do it. After nineteen years of imprisonment, he escapes and flees to Mexico. Andy uses soft and stealthy methods to reach his goals. Probably because of his background as a banker, he's able to think long-term and knows that small actions in the present will eventually lead to big changes in the future. He also loved geology, which is, as the film puts it, "a study of pressure and time."

By being friendly and helpful and using his intelligence, he's able to become a trustee of the corrupt and heartless prison warden Samuel Norton and enjoys several privileges. By sending a letter to the state senate every week for six years, he's been able to get funding for a prison library. Eventually, Andy escapes through a tunnel he dug using a small hammer, which he had hidden in a bible. It takes him nineteen years to dig that tunnel, a project he hides behind a poster of a pin-up girl. With his soft and patient approach, he conquered not only a thick, concrete wall but also the prison's authority.

His escape, however, is explosive. He rushes into the tunnel, gets on the other side, breaks a sewer pipe, crawls through five hundred yards of excrement, cashes in, exposes the warden to the media, and flees to Mexico. Thus, he doesn't abstain from using force completely; he just saves it for the right opportunity, which took him nineteen years of softness to create.

3) Seeing the silver lining

To be like water means that we're able to adapt to different circumstances. Every situation has something positive to it. In still water, the dust can settle so that it becomes clear. Streaming water passes different places and sceneries and nurtures the things that it encounters. In the yang-society we live in, we only seem to value one part of human existence, which is the active part that revolves around achievement, speed, and success.

We get educated, take on a lot of responsibility in regard to work and family, try to get rich and do it as quickly as possible, and judge each other as "human doings" rather than human beings. Being useless, or stupid, or ugly, or poor, is generally considered undesirable. But if we master the flexibility of finding the positive in the negative, we'll realize that these undesired characteristics have positive aspects to them. It's just a matter of perception. For example, being poor means less money and possessions to worry about, and being ugly means that we're less likely to end up in a string of abusive relationships and that people like us for our personality instead of our looks.

Life is characterized by softness, and softness is strength. Soft things don't break easily because they can bend and yield, unlike brittle and rigid ones. Even the hardest of rock can be overcome by the gentleness of water. Hence, a famous actor, philosopher, and martial artist once said: "Don't get set into one form, adapt it and build your own, and let it grow, be like water."[53]

---

[53] A famous quote by Bruce Lee, from *Bruce Lee: A Warrior's Story*

Taoist Sages on Inner Peace

Laozi

If you can empty your mind of all thoughts
your heart will embrace the tranquility of peace.

Laozi, *Tao Te Ching*, chapter 16

There's no proof that Laozi truly ever lived, but if he did, it should have been somewhere around the 5th and 6th century B.C., which makes him a contemporary of Confucius. Nevertheless, as mentioned earlier, the legendary philosopher Laozi is traditionally credited with writing the *Tao Te Ching*, the foundational text of Taoism. However, the *Tao Te Ching* remains a mysterious work—not only is there no consensus on when it was written (though it likely dates to the late Warring States period), but even the existence of Laozi himself is disputed.

One thing is certain: the profundity of the *Tao Te Ching* has left its mark on humanity to this day. It's also the most translated work in world literature after the Bible. Laozi wrote about themes such as virtue, non-action, the Tao, and moderation, but also about warfare and ruling a country. The *Tao Te Ching* seems to be written for a ruler, although it also contains insights that can benefit anyone. Many of Laozi's teachings are timeless. And I believe his wisdom is particularly valuable for today's stressed-out, accomplishment-driven society, which is what this chapter is aimed toward.

1) Achievement society

We live in a world where striving is the norm. It's all about achievement, optimal performance, and self-optimization. We've become our own taskmasters, continuously pushing ourselves to achieve more and move faster. We live in a world where stress, burnout, depression, and anxiety have become embedded in the fabric of our daily lives. And as these phenomena become more prevalent and severe, we're on our way from collective self-exploitation to collective self-destruction. Today's society is a Taoist's nightmare. It's so disconnected from the natural flow of life, so obsessed with control, status, consumption, and materialism that we've forgotten how to be at peace.

I once published a video on Byung-Chul Han, the German-Korean philosopher who describes our era as an "achievement society," where we, as achievement subjects, have become our own taskmasters—driving ourselves to accomplish more and more, often to the point of burnout. The insanity of today's system is putting endless strain on its people.

From an imperative to achieve, we're stretching ourselves beyond our means, running endlessly through rat races, and self-optimizing in every area that we possibly can. It's like just having a PhD isn't enough: we feel we need to have a PhD, a six-pack, a perfect marriage, an interesting and amazing social circle, and to be running marathons, traveling, and displaying all these things on social media. In a stressful, insane world where we encourage each other to self-exploit, it's difficult to truly relax.

Many go to bed tormented by worries about the future and wake up with their mind filled with endless tasks and to-do lists. Our lives have become a collection of sprints from task to task, with hardly any time for reflection. Contemplation is a waste of time. Boredom is evil. Idleness is a sin. We should be grinding, always becoming better versions of ourselves. We should always be headed toward the prize. But the ongoing grind without proper moments of non-action will eventually wear us down.

2) The suffering of attachment

What's so refreshing about Laozi's teachings is that they invite us to go in the opposite direction. Laozi asks us what's more important: fame and wealth, or ourselves—how we feel, our contentment, and our inner peace?

Fame can be pleasurable, especially for those who like attention, but there are many downsides as well, and it's difficult to attain and maintain. Just look at those who have it, get attached to it, and do the craziest things, sometimes out of desperation, to stay relevant. And what about money? Money is convenient, for sure. But does money itself make us happy?

Fame or self: Which matters more?
Self or wealth: Which is more precious?
Gain or loss: Which is more painful?
He who is attached to things will suffer much.
He who saves will suffer heavy loss.
A contented man is never disappointed.
He who knows when to stop
does not find himself in trouble.
He will stay forever safe.

Laozi, *Tao Te Ching*, chapter 44 (Gia-fu Feng and Jane English)

According to Laozi, it doesn't. Ultimately, our happiness and contentment don't depend on all these outside factors. Contentment lies within. It's the absence of lack, the feeling that the way things are is perfectly fine, which doesn't require all the stuff society tells us we should have; we might as well let go of it and focus on cultivating contentment with less. The James Legge translation of the same verse states:

Be content with what you have;
rejoice in the way things are.
When you realize there is nothing lacking,
the whole world belongs to you.

Laozi, *Tao Te Ching*, chapter 44 (James Legge)

3) Embracing simplicity

It's no surprise that we're always so busy. Our world offers so many possibilities, so many paths to take, and so many ways to improve ourselves, achieve more, attain more, buy more, and experience more. The paradox of choice alone is already a source of stress and exhaustion. Let's contemplate the following words by Laozi:

If you over-esteem talented individuals,
people will become overly competitive.
If you overvalue possessions,
people will begin to steal.
Do not display your treasures
or people will become envious.

Laozi, *Tao Te Ching*, chapter 3

This simple verse illustrates the problem with our achievement-oriented society. First of all, we overestimate talent and accomplishment, so people behave accordingly. It's all about achievement. It's all about showing how great we are compared to others. And yes, people *have* become overly competitive in today's world. In almost everything, we find competition nowadays, be it in schools, workplaces, or social media. The common good isn't important anymore; it's all about individual success and ego, as we have become entrepreneurs of ourselves.

Can't we say the same thing about possessions? Aren't these the indicators of success we try to attain, the proof of being a successful achievement subject? "People begin to steal," argues Laozi, which is true, but not only that. People act in unethical, immoral ways to get what they want, kicking others down to get higher up. Needless to say, narcissism is prevalent. Being a narcissist pays.

Also, Laozi observed that showing off our material possessions makes people envious, which only attracts trouble and leads to more stress. "The more wealth you possess, the harder it is to protect it,"[54] he argued.

If we want to let go of all these stresses, embracing simplicity may be a wise move. What if we're free from all these modern-day desires? What if we don't feel the need to self-optimize in so many different areas? How about *not* being well-rounded? How about *not* standing out? How about *not* being successful according to societal standards? How tranquil would our lives be if we ignored today's society's imperatives and were content with less?

4) Balance over self-exploitation

In earlier chapters, we've explored the idea of swimming against the stream and letting oneself float along with it.

---

[54] Laozi, *Tao Te Ching*, chapter 9

The idea is simple: if we swim against the stream, we put in lots of effort to get somewhere, but sometimes, we don't even reach our goal. One thing is certain: we become exhausted. Therefore, Laozi repeatedly mentions the power of non-doing.

If we were aware of the workings of the universe, we would see how our actions are counterproductive. For example, overstretching ourselves in our pursuit of unending self-optimization and self-improvement may cause us to constantly push ourselves toward collapse, which isn't a very stable way of living. As Laozi observed, *"Those who stand on tiptoes do not stand firmly."*[55]

Hence, Laozi also advises his readers to be wary about taking the highest position. The tallest trees catch the most wind. And when we're at the top, it takes a tremendous amount of effort to stay there because many want the top position. It's stressful compared to the lower regions, in which one lives more privately, with less competition, fewer enemies, and generally, less effort. In short, we're standing more firmly on the ground in the lower position.

Laozi also has a message for the go-getters among us who try to rush themselves to the top and end up falling for get-rich-quick schemes, which are often formulas for failure and wasted energy: "Those who rush ahead don't

---

[55] Laozi, *Tao Te Ching*, chapter 24

get very far,"[56] he wrote. We could also apply this to multitasking (the act of doing several things simultaneously), which ultimately inhibits our ability to perform really well at one task or create something of substance.

Unfortunately, we live in a society that's always in a rush. We're rushing to get things done, rushing to get wealthy, even rushing to self-improve. Learn Spanish in six days! Get a six-pack in a week! Become a millionaire by drop-shipping and retire before you're twenty-five! Most of the time, these things don't work.

So, why the rush? Why the overstretching? Why live on the edge of exhaustion all the time? We're not doing ourselves a favor. Yet, society commands us to always be busy. Rushing and grinding, no matter if we're swimming against the stream. Doing is a virtue. Hence, we have offices full of people who are more concerned with showing that they're productive than actually producing something. Also, things like substance, balance, patience, careful consideration, and slow but steady progress aren't exactly celebrated. But these are the fundamentals to a robust, substantial form of success.

What if we abandon the societal expectation of stretching ourselves beyond our means and quick but unsubstantial status and success? "Those who try to outshine others dim their own light,"[57] wrote Laozi. What

---

[56] Laozi, *Tao Te Ching*, chapter 24
[57] Laozi, *Tao Te Ching*, chapter 24

if we put substance over status and balance over self-exploitation? What if we let go of what philosopher Alain de Botton calls "Status Anxiety," which is the anxiety that comes from comparing oneself to others and worrying that we are falling short of society's expectations?

5) Stop controlling everything

We just have to contemplate the vastness of the universe to realize how powerless we are as fragile humans living on a desolate rock somewhere on the outskirts of the Milky Way galaxy. Perhaps for that very reason, we're obsessed with control, as we incessantly try to control our environment and ourselves. Laozi wrote:

Do you want to rule the world and control it?
I don't think it can ever be done.
The world is sacred vessel
and it can not be controlled.
You will only it make it worse if you try.
It may slip through your fingers and disappear.

Laozi, *Tao Te Ching*, chapter 3

There are many ways we try to control our environment and ourselves. For example, we wish to be safe, and we believe that accumulating a lot of money and having ten security cameras around the house will ensure that. We want to be perceived highly in the eyes of others, so we put everything in place to make sure those in proximity think highly of us. We want to keep our jobs, so we answer to all of our employers' whims so we won't get fired and worry about keeping our jobs day and night. But we're *never* safe.

We can't control other people's opinions. We can't command our boss's attitude toward us. Once we accept this, we'll see we're wasting time doing so. We might even harm ourselves if we hold on to the illusion: we'll experience stress, and the universe might work against us, as it doesn't let itself be controlled. Why not focus on what we can control, which is our ability to find inner peace amid chaos? But to do so, we'll have to be willing to let that chaos—that insanity we're so wrapped up in–be.

Liezi

Lieh Yokuo, also known as Liezi or Master Lie, is attributed as the author of the eponymous ancient Taoist text of the same name, the *Liezi.* This book contains many stories with philosophical themes like the nature of reality, the purpose of life, and the workings of the mind. One theme that runs like a thread through it is the tendency of human beings to stand in their own way and thereby sabotage a spontaneous, effortless mode of living.

Even though there's a debate among scholars whether or not Liezi truly existed as a person, the text is considered the third most important scripture in Taoism, after the *Tao Te Ching* and the *Zhuangzi.* Zhuangzi describes Liezi as the sage who rode the wind with an admirable indifference to external things, and thus, in his lightness, he was free from all desires to pursue the things that supposedly make us happy.

1) The Sage Who Rode the Wind

The *Liezi* tells how this Taoist sage let go of the weight of the world and became so light that he was able to ride the wind and float with the clouds. This happened after a period of disciplining his body and mind, during which he let go of conceptions of right and wrong. After years of practice, Liezi experienced that the barrier between himself and the outside world had disappeared, as had the heaviness of his bones and flesh. He stated: *"Without knowing it, I was being carried by the wind. Drifting here and there, I did not know whether I rode on the wind or the wind rode on me.*[58] *"*

Now, riding the wind isn't to be taken literally. It's a metaphor for a "mental state" that we can experience, according to the Taoist sages, in which we move lightly through life as if we're floating. We ride the wind when external circumstances don't weigh us down because we don't resist them but live in harmony with them. Laozi and Zhuangzi *also* point to this state in their unique ways. Zhuangzi tells us to let our minds wander in the pure and simple, to be one with the infinite, and let all things take their course. Laozi describes it as becoming "one with the dust" and asserts that those who do cannot be benefitted nor harmed, approached nor alienated, made noble nor suffer disgrace. Imagine how light life would be if nothing in the universe could harm us.

2) The Yellow Emperor

We can find a beautiful description of this state of "riding the wind" in a story[59] about the Yellow Emperor, who

---

[58] Wong, Eva. *Lieh-tzu: A Taoist Guide to Practical Living* (Shambhala Dragon Editions) (p. 69). Shambhala.

[59] You'll find this story in the book *Lieh-Tzu: A Practical Guide to Taoist Living* by Eva Wong, chapter 12: The yellow emperor visits the immortal lands

suffered ill health and restlessness after ruling the country for many years. For many years, he had pushed himself anxiously, governing the country closely to the greatest detail. But when he decided to take a break from his duties, he indulged in the greatest pleasures to satisfy the senses. But these modes of life left him exhausted and jaded. The Yellow Emperor stated: *"I pampered myself too much, and then pushed myself too hard. No wonder I lost my health and my inner peace."*[60]

So, the Yellow Emperor decided to distance himself from his imperial duties and stay away from the sensual pleasures that he had previously indulged in. He retreated to his private quarters to engage in what the Taoists call "the fasting of the heart." This refers to the art of freeing oneself from earthly desires so that the body synchronizes with the natural course of things.

And thus, for three months, the Yellow Emperor abstained from intervention in government and subdued the senses, but it seemed that he wanted results too quickly. Mind you that it took Liezi many, many years before he was able to ride the wind, so was it realistic to expect results so fast?

The Yellow Emperor had worn himself out after a relatively short time of isolation. Exhausted, he fell asleep during the day and dreamed about a journey to a faraway

---

[60] Wong, Eva. Lieh-tzu: A Taoist Guide to Practical Living (Shambhala Dragon Editions) (p. 65). Shambhala.

kingdom. This kingdom had no ruler; it simply went on by itself. Its people didn't have cravings and desires outside of their instincts and weren't attached to life nor averse to death.

They were without preference and prejudice. Hence, love and hate didn't occur, and things like attraction, repulsion, wanting, disliking, gain, and loss were all alien to these people who seemed to be consistently unaffected by external circumstances, and it was as if they moved about like gods.

Water had no power to drown them, nor fire to burn; cuts and blows caused them neither injury nor pain, scratching or tickling could not make them itch. They bestrode the air as though treading on solid earth; they were cradled in space as though resting in a bed.[61]

After his dream, the Yellow Emperor felt enlightened. He told his ministers that he now comprehended "the Way" but also understood that the Way cannot be perceived by the senses nor explained by words. He realized that one cannot become enlightened by conscious thinking and effort, but rather that it's something that happens spontaneously. In his case: in a dream that occurred after he stopped trying. Great orderliness followed in the empire, and when the Yellow

---

[61] *Taoist Teachings Translated from the Book of Lieh-Tzü* (Lionel Giles), Book II: The Yellow Emperor

Emperor passed away, the people mourned his death for two hundred years.

3) How to Ride the Wind

The question is, of course, how can one become as light as a Taoist sage and ride the wind? The *Liezi* gives us several hints on how to pull this off. However, there's a paradoxical nature to it.

On the one hand, there's a certain practice involved in letting go of earthly desires, as well as the numerous categories and ideas created by the mind. On the other hand, enlightenment seems to happen suddenly. In the case of the sage Liezi, it took years, but the Yellow Emperor was enlightened after just a couple of months. In both cases, the change occurred when, during their practice, they reached a state of non-practice.

So, this sudden, spontaneous moment when one's body ceases to be heavy and begins to float along with the wind like the seeds of a dandelion is aligned with the Taoist idea of "doing without doing" or "non-action."

It's only when we stop striving, stop making an effort, quit going somewhere, and stop fighting against the world that we get where we want to be: in the flow state, in which we float along with nature's current entirely instead of resisting it. This, according to Laozi, is how one achieves mastery of the world.

One who seeks knowledge
learns something new every day.
One who seeks the Tao
unlearns something new every day.
Less and less remains
until you arrive at non-action.
When you arrive at non-action,
nothing will be left undone.

Mastery of the world is achieved
by letting things take their natural course.
You cannot master the world
by changing the natural way.

Laozi, *Tao Te Ching*, 48

Liezi explained to his disciple, a man named Yin-sheng, what he went through before he became as light as a feather. He mentioned that after letting go of the notions of right and wrong, there was no barrier between himself and the outside world. So, it seems that he stopped experiencing the separateness that was previously created by the mind. And that it's that sense of separateness that causes us to feel heavy and suffer.

One day, *Liezi* asked the Taoist sage Wen Tzu why an enlightened person cannot be drowned by water nor burned by fire. Wen Tzu explained that even though we separate things based on their external features, everything is fundamentally the same, as everything comes from the same origin.

So, when we cease to see ourselves separated from water, it won't drown us. And when we cease to see ourselves separated from fire, it won't burn us. Hence, the man who danced in the fire said: *"What are rocks, what are flames? I don't know what you're talking about."*[62]

Like the story about riding the wind, these examples can be used as metaphors for how we can free ourselves from being affected by the world around us. Again, these shouldn't be taken too literally, and deeper meaning can be found if we read the whole second book, which tells us about the many miracles that people are capable of when they are in the flow state as well as (which is perhaps even *more* important) how people tend to *lose* these abilities.

A farmer named Shang jumped from the highest cliffs without breaking a bone, obtained jewels from the deepest rivers, and rescued bundles of silk out of a burning building. He did all of this in pure spontaneity, without hesitation or fear, and without a desire for profit or a good reputation among his kinsmen. Only when he started thinking about the risks did he discover what it was like to be afraid and began to doubt his capabilities. Hence, he decided to never do these things again.

---

[62] Wong, Eva. *Lieh-tzu: A Taoist Guide to Practical Living* (Shambhala Dragon Editions) (p. 83). Shambhala.

So, when farmer Shang jumped into the arena of life without reluctance, he wasn't held back by doubt because he had nothing to gain or lose. He embarked on the natural flow of life and just did what he did. But from the very moment that his mind took over, he was standing in his own way.

Anxious about the terrible fate he could meet at the end of the river stream, he started holding on to rocks and branches. And thus, his body became a heavy burden, as opposed to the weightlessness he experienced when he still flowed along with the stream. Or as philosopher Alan Watts stated when reflecting on Liezi:

What is this, then; weightlessness? It means, partly, that you're not moving around in constant opposition to yourself. Most people move in constant opposition to themselves because they are afraid that, if they don't oppose themselves all the time, something awful will happen.[63]

Liezi shows us that only when we transcend the duality of life—things like gain and loss, attraction and repulsion, wonderful and awful—can we become truly indifferent and start acting for no other reason than the action itself. Because what's to fear when the outcome is irrelevant?

---

[63] Watts, A. (n.d.-b). Swimming headless. The Library. https://www.organism.earth/library/document/swimming-headless

When we achieve this state, we don't swim in the water, but become the water, and we aren't burned by fire, but we become the fire itself. And before we know it, on a stormy day, we may suddenly start riding the wind.

Zhuangzi

Centuries ago, the Taoist philosopher Zhuangzi sat by a river, watching the water flow, his fishing rod resting beside him. Unexpectedly, two vice-chancellors appeared before him, having been dispatched by the Prince of Chu to offer Zhuangzi the esteemed position of prime minister.

Without a worry on his face, Zhuangzi continued to observe the river's motion. He said to his visitors: "I've heard of a sacred turtle that was removed from its natural habitat, only for its shell to be draped in silk and put on display in the royal palace. Now, let me ask you: Which do you think is preferable? To be worshipped by the masses in the company of royalty, sacrificed as a lifeless object, or to live as an ordinary turtle, freely dragging its tail through the mud?" After a moment of contemplation, one of the vice-chancellors said: "For the turtle's well-being, it is surely better to live and drag its tail in the mud."

"Ah," said Zhuangzi, "there you have it. Please return to your prince and tell him that I prefer to remain here, dragging my tail in the mud."

This story[64] about Zhuangzi, who rejected a powerful position to maintain his peaceful, obscure life by the riverside, characterizes the vibe surrounding the eponymous philosophical work, the *Zhuangzi*.

---

[64] This story is a loose adaptation from chapter 17 "An Autumn Flood" (Outer chapters) of the *Zhuangzi*

As a character, Zhuangzi embodies a sense of calm, playfulness, and humility. As a philosopher, he saw the world differently. Compared to many of his contemporaries, Zhuangzi managed to break through conventions, let go of fixed views, and look beyond the human scope and understanding of right and wrong. He saw the usefulness in uselessness, beauty in ugliness, and order in chaos. And by seeing and approaching the world in his unique and, sometimes, inverted ways, he exudes a strong sense of contentment and ease in the midst of an ever-changing and often chaotic existence.

Zhuangzi reminds us to go with the flow and see the silver lining of whatever happens. He didn't take life too seriously and embraced living spontaneously. Instead of living according to a set of constraining, fixed, dogmatic rules, like the Confucianists with their rituals and etiquette, Zhuangzi preferred an existence in harmony with nature and in agreement with Tao, the underlying principle of the universe.

1) Zhuangzi's life

Zhuangzi, both the philosopher and the text bearing his name, have left a lasting mark on Chinese culture. Living around the 4th century BCE, during the Warring States period, the *Zhuangzi* has become synonymous with parables and anecdotes that show the joy of simplicity, the relativity of all things, and the harmony and ease achieved by aligning oneself with the all-encompassing force known as Tao. Zhuangzi's teachings diverge from Confucianism, which is a social and ethical philosophy—or social ritual—that focuses on teaching morality, maintaining social hierarchy, and establishing strict codes of conduct.

While Confucianism can be seen as effective, in the eyes of the Taoist sages, it's inflexible and artificial. Zhuangzi's teachings, on the other hand, come across as playful and unconfined. He mocks rigid principles, structured social order, hierarchy, and any form of dogmatic thought and practice. After all, the universe is ever-changing, our views of reality are extremely limited, and so the only true experience of life is through direct, spontaneous engagement with the present moment, *not* through some fixed, man-made collection of beliefs and convictions.

The stories in the *Zhuangzi* show this typical Taoist playfulness and open-mindedness in viewing and approaching the world, and they put emphasis on subjective experience rather than a rigid set of views and ideas on "how things should be." Take, for example, probably the most famous story from the *Zhuangzi*, the "Butterfly Dream,"[65] which shows how one's whole reality and identity can change through subjective

---

[65] You'll find this story in the *Zhuangzi*, Inner Chapters, Chapter 2: Discussion on making all things equal

experience, questioning the validity and existence of objective reality altogether. Or, take the lesser-known story about the "Useless Tree,"[66] which shows how even the most useless things have a place in the world and how every disadvantage often comes with a hidden advantage. We'll explore this story later in this essay. Also, Zhuangzi encouraged living in harmony with nature, or the natural flow of existence, and not going against it or altering it. He stated:

When all men do not carry their nature beyond its normal condition, nor alter its characteristics, the good government of the world is secured.[67]

Like his predecessor Laozi, the life of this ancient philosopher is veiled in mystery. Despite the many stories about him and attributed to him, did he actually exist? And if so, what was his role in writing and compiling the book that carries his name? Some scholars argue that Zhuangzi was a real historical figure, while others believe that he may be a fictional character or a composite of several philosophers. Ultimately, the question of Zhuangzi's historical existence remains open and may never be definitively resolved.

2) It's all relative

---

[66] You'll find this story in the *Zhuangzi*, Outer Chapters, Chapter 20: The mountain tree

[67] *The Writings of Chuang Tzu* (James Legge), Chapter 11: Letting Be, and Exercising Forbearance

One day, Nie Que and Wang Ni took a stroll along the waterfront.[68] Their eyes fell upon a gathering of men, utterly entranced by a stunning woman who graced the area with her presence. "She is so gorgeous," Nie Que said. As the pair continued their walk, Wang Ni observed how the fish in the river and the birds in the sky would hastily flee at the sight of the woman. Turning to Nie Que, Wang Ni remarked, "Observe how the fish and birds are disturbed by this woman's presence, while humans find her alluring and simply can't keep their eyes off her." Nie Que nodded, and Wang Ni added, "This illustrates how beauty is a matter of perspective. What one creature finds captivating may not hold the same appeal for another. Which of these beings knows what is truly beautiful in the world? Indeed, beauty lies in the eye of the beholder."

Zhuangzi underscores the relativity of not only beauty but of all things in the world. Our perceptions and judgments don't make facts.[69] In regard to beauty, our perceptions and judgments are shaped by factors like individual experiences, cultural norms, time periods, and environments. However, there is also scientific data showing that across different cultures and time periods, people consider specific traits beautiful, like

---

[68] This story is a loose adaptation of a conversation between Nie Que and Wang Ni, recorded in chapter 2 (Discussion on making all things equal) in the *Zhuangzi.*

[69] Zhuangzi goes into this particularly in the *Zhuangzi,* chapter 2: Discussion on making all things equal

youthfulness, symmetrical faces, clear skin, and physical fitness.

Could we then speak of objective beauty? Even if the woman at the waterfront would be considered attractive by all humans, then, according to Zhuangzi, we still cannot say she's objectively beautiful. The fishes and birds found her atrocious. A dog probably doesn't even care about or notice her beauty. And what could we say about trees and plants? Even though it's disputed whether these organisms are sentient or not, if they are, they may be utterly indifferent to how she looks in the eyes of men. So, what we might call "universal" beauty standards are, in reality, just human beauty standards; they're only true in the human experience.

The thought that many (if not all) things are relative can be a source of calm. Our ideas, how important and "true" they may seem, are nothing more than the perspectives coming from a species living on a tiny little dot in an endless universe. From a human perspective, what appears vast in size may seem minuscule when viewed from the vantage point of a star. Likewise, actions deemed immoral and unethical within human society may not hold the same negative connotations when considered through the eyes of a hungry lion.

The realization that everything is relative can lead to a more carefree approach to life as we learn to let go of rigid beliefs and put subjective experiences, opinions, personal tastes, and views in perspective. They aren't as definitive and all-encompassing as they might seem. So, the less reason we have to cling to them and take them so darn seriously.

3) Spontaneity & wu wei

One day, Cook Ding demonstrated his exceptional butchery skills by carving an ox, his blade gliding effortlessly through the meat without dulling.[70] In awe, a nobleman asked how he managed such mastery, to which Cook Ding explained that he relied on *wu wei* (or effortless action) by following the natural order of things and following his instinct. Thus, his craft became an elegant dance, harmonious with the universe and unencumbered by resistance and over-intellectualizing his actions.

As mentioned previously, wu wei is a central concept within Taoism, often translated as non-doing, doing nothing, and effortless action. If we're engaged in a specific activity, we may experience being "in the zone," so to speak, in which our intellectual activity is minimal, and whatever we're doing seems to go automatically without thinking and effort. When we're in the zone, there's hardly any worry about the future or reminiscing the past; it's pure clarity and immersion in our actions,

---

[70] You'll find the famous story of Cook Ding in the *Zhuangzi*, Chapter 3: The secret of caring for life

like a dancer becoming the dance or a painter becoming the painting.

Cook Ding achieved wu wei after years of practice, so he was able to let his intuition (or the natural flow) take over. He stated:

When I first began to cut up an ox, I saw nothing but the (entire) carcass. After three years I ceased to see it as a whole. Now I deal with it in a spirit-like manner, and do not look at it with my eyes. The use of my senses is discarded, and my spirit acts as it wills.[71]

4) Usefulness of uselessness

Huizi complained to Zhuangzi about a large tree that was totally unfit to use to make wooden planks. The tree was extremely crooked; the main trunk was gnarled and knotted, and the branches were twisted. Carpenters could not use the tree, as opposed to the straight trees, so the woodcutters never touched it. Then, Zhuangzi said:

Have you ever observed the wildcat? It crouches concealed and waits for its prey to wander in range – then it springs left or right, heedless of heights and chasms. And yet wildcats spring our traps and die in our nets. Or

---

[71] *The Writings of Chuang Tzu* (James Legge), Chapter 3: Nourishing the Lord of Life (to prevent confusion: the Legge version has different names for the titles than the translation by Burton Watson)

take the yak, big as a cloud hung from the sky – it's skilled at being huge, but it can't even catch a rat. Now you have this big tree but its uselessness is a trouble to you. Why don't you plant it in the village and amble beside it doing nothing at all, or wander free and easy lying asleep beneath it? No ax will ever cut short its life, nothing will ever harm it. If there's no use for it, what hardship could ever befall it?[72]

Many people overlook the usefulness of uselessness. It seems we're only interested in what's useful while scorning what we deem useless. But the crooked tree story shows that seemingly useless things can be very useful; the tree became a spot to relax, have a romantic time with a lover, and hide from the sun, and eventually, people considered it a holy place because of its longevity and unique shape. Moreover, the perceived uselessness (from a human standpoint, being useful as a tree for wooden planks) served as a ticket for survival, as people were not motivated to cut it down.

But there's more to the usefulness of uselessness. From the Taoist point of view, what we perceive as useless is necessary for things to function. As Laozi mentioned, everything is interdependent. There can't be high without low, there can't be before without after, and

---

[72] *Zhuangzi: The Inner Chapters* (translated by Robert Eno), Chapter 1: Free and easy wandering

reasoning from the same principle, there can't be usefulness without uselessness. A cup cannot be used without the empty space within it. A door is useless without the emptiness through which one can walk. The same sentiment is shared in the *Zhuangzi*, in which the philosopher argued that even though only a few acres of the Earth's surface are suitable for farmland, these pieces of farmland wouldn't serve any purpose, nor would they "operate" if the rest of the Earth didn't exist.

If we ever feel useless (or are considered useless), we can always think of the usefulness of uselessness. Useful people can't be useful without those who have no use within a specific context. There can't be doctors without patients; there can't be gossipers without despicable people to gossip and complain about. For example, the philosophical entertainer Alan Watts mentioned in one of his talks that the people we tend to complain about have a function, which is not only that they generate a great portion of our conversation but also that they are a reference point to make ourselves feel better than others. The reason there are "good people" is that there are "bad people"; without bad people, or at least the concept of what makes a bad person, good people would not exist. If there isn't "bad," what makes something else "good?" So, if you're perceived as a bad, useless person, you can always think: "Well, at least I make others feel good about themselves."

5) Accepting impermanence

The impermanent nature of the universe is another topic Zhuangzi seems to be concerned with. Once, the Taoist sage demonstrated how he embraced the ever-changing nature of life when his wife passed away. His friend Huizi paid him a visit to offer condolences and was taken aback to find Zhuangzi sitting on the ground, tapping on a basin and singing.

Huizi couldn't help but express his bewilderment, questioning Zhuangzi's seemingly inappropriate behavior. Zhuangzi, in his typically calm and insightful manner, explained to Huizi that he was initially indeed saddened by his wife's passing. However, he soon began to contemplate the nature of her existence. Before she was born, she had neither life nor form, and even before that, she didn't even have breath. Over time, changes occurred, giving rise to breath, form, life, and eventually, her death.

Zhuangzi recognized that these transformations were as natural as the progression of the seasons, and her death was just another part of this cosmic dance. As he gazed upon her peaceful face, Zhuangzi understood that to weep and wail would be to reject the inherent impermanence of life. Instead, he chose to celebrate the ever-changing nature of existence and embrace the ebb and flow of life's journey. In doing so, Zhuangzi showed us that by accepting the impermanence of all things, we can more easily cope with life's many transformations: the loss of loved ones, the aging of our bodies, gain and loss, fame and disrepute.

Just before Zhuangzi died, he stopped his disciples from organizing a magnificent funeral. "What more is necessary for a proper goodbye than Heaven and Earth as a coffin, the stars and planets as decorations, and all beings present as company?" he stated. But his disciples protested, arguing that without a coffin and burial, the crows and vultures would eat their beloved sage. Once again demonstrating his carefree and playful attitude, Zhuangzi replied: "Above ground, crows and vultures will consume me, while below ground, ants and worms will feast upon me. In both situations, I will be devoured. What makes you favor ants and worms so much?"[73]

---

[73] This story, written in my own words, is from chapter 32: Lie Yukoo (Outer chapters) of the *Zhuangzi*

Printed in Great Britain
by Amazon

60318290R00099